Blood
on the
Streets

1916 & The Battle for Mount Street Bridge

MERCIER PRESS
Douglas Village, Cork
www.mercierpress.ie

Trade enquiries to:
Columba Mercier Distribution, 55a Spruce Avenue, Stillorgan
Industrial Park, Blackrock, County Dublin

ISBN: 978 1 85635 576 6

10 9 8 7 6 5 4 3 2 1

Mercier Press receives financial assistance from the Arts
Council/An Chomhairle Ealaíon

Printed and bound in the EU.

PAUL O'BRIEN

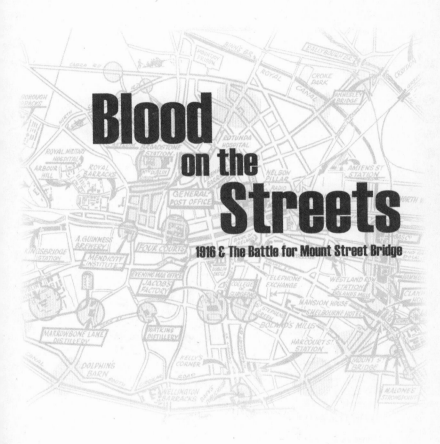

Blood on the Streets

1916 & The Battle for Mount Street Bridge

MERCIER PRESS
WHAT YOU NEED TO READ

1 Boland's Bakery
2 Clanwilliam House
3 Mount St. Bridge
4 Parochial Hall
5 25 Northumberland Rd.
6 School
7 Barracks

Landsdowne Road Station

Dublin, Wicklow and Wexford Railway

Shelbourne Road

Mount Canal Street

Landsdowne Lane

Landsdowne Road

Northumberland Road

Pembroke Road

Canal Docks

Grand Canal Quay

Grand Canal Street

Warrington Place

Haddington Road

Canal

Lower Mount Street

Street

Contents

FOREWORD   9

PRELUDE   11

EASTER MONDAY, 24 APRIL 1916   18

TUESDAY, 25 APRIL 1916   27

WEDNESDAY, 26 APRIL 1916 MORNING   34

WEDNESDAY, 26 APRIL 1916 EARLY AFTERNOON   42

WEDNESDAY, 26 APRIL 1916 MID AFTERNOON   53

WEDNESDAY, 26 APRIL 1916 EVENING   61

WEDNESDAY, 26 APRIL 1916 THE FINAL HOUR   73

WEDNESDAY, 26 APRIL 1916 NIGHTFALL   78

MAY 1916 – EXECUTIONS AT KILMAINHAM GAOL   84

AFTERMATH 91

**APRIL 1916 – MILITARY SUCCESS AND
MILITARY FAILURE** 100

**TODAY – LET US NOT BE FORGOTTEN
NÁ LIG SINN i nDEARMAD** 112

EPILOGUE 118

NOTES 119

INDEX 123

Acknowledgements

This book could not have been written without the assistance and co-operation of John McGuiggan, barrister at law. Unrestricted access was granted to me on valuable material that he uncovered during his research and his encouragement and helpful suggestions contributed greatly to the completion of this work.

I am deeply indebted to Sue Sutton for her research in the British Military Archives at Kew in London, to Elizabeth Gillis for providing information on the Irish Volunteers and to Dr. Mike Briggs and Andrew D. Hesketh for material on the Sherwood Foresters.

Grateful thanks are also due to the staff of The National Library, Dublin, Military Archives, Dublin, University College Dublin Archives, Kilmainham Gaol Archives, the Office of Public Works, Cliff Houseley of the Sherwood Foresters Museum, Eoin Purcell and the staff of Mercier Press.

My appreciation to John Finlay and Stan O'Reilly of the Wicklow Historical Society for granting permission to quote from diaries held by Debbie and Jack Buckley.

My thanks and appreciation to David Duff and Bernard Stanford of the Irish Museum of Modern Art for granting me access to Bully's Acre Graveyard.

My thanks to the following for their encouragement

and advice, Mary Montaut, Wayne Fitzgerald, Gerry Kelly, Cyril Wall, Paul Turnell, David Borril, Michael O' Doiblín, Phyl Mason, John Mannion, Barry Keogh, my parents for their continued support and to my fiancée Marian McLaughlin who kindly and patiently assisted me in this venture.

This book has been written using available historical records both in Ireland and in England. I apologise if I have omitted anyone who should have been included and I would like to invite them to make me aware of these for any future updated edition.

My thanks are due to all those who provided help and information in the course of writing this book.

FOREWORD

During the summer months of 2001, I was researching Dublin's oldest graveyard, Bully's Acre. This cemetery is located within the grounds of the Royal Hospital Kilmainham, the former retirement home for soldiers who had served in the British army. The graveyard consists of an officers' burial ground as well as a plot for soldiers who held the rank up to warrant officer. These are separated by a larger public area commonly known as Bully's Acre. In the graveyard for the lower ranks, among the fallen headstones, brambles and weeds can be found two Commonwealth war grave headstones belonging to men of the Nottingham and Derbyshire regiments. They commemorate two young British soldiers who had fallen during the rebellion of Easter 1916. I was curious to find out more about these soldiers, their regiment and the action that had brought them to Dublin city. Researching these lonely graves, I discovered that these men had fallen in one of the bloodiest and perhaps the most successful engagements fought by the Irish Volunteers during Easter week 1916.

The battle of Mount Street Bridge may be considered controversial from both British and Irish viewpoints, and it raises many unanswered questions. The result of the battle was that the British crown forces suffered their heaviest losses during the Rising, something that would prove an embarrassment to the British army and to the British government. Questions arose with regards to the military strategy and tactics deployed by the British army and whether the losses they suffered could have been avoided.

With regard to the Irish Volunteers, one must also question, for example, why their commanding officer was reluctant to send reinforcements to the beleaguered section defending Mount Street.

This book is not an attempt to retell the complete history of the 1916 Rising, but it does attempt to recount one particular episode that unfolded in a suburb of Dublin. It reveals the gallant heroism of a handful of Irishmen who held almost two battalions at bay as Ireland was declared a republic. Many books have already been written on the rebellion of 1916 and each of these publications includes a section on the battle of Mount Street, but I hope that this book will dispel many of the myths that have been created over the decades and will act as a token of remembrance to those extraordinary men on both sides who fought and died for what they believed was freedom.

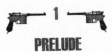

1
PRELUDE

At the beginning of the twentieth century, Ireland formed part of the United Kingdom of Great Britain and Ireland, a connection that shaped the politics and administration of the country. Since the thirteenth century Ireland had been considered a separate kingdom, with its own parliament in Dublin. However, in 1801, with the implementation of the Act of Union, Ireland's legal independence was removed. The Irish parliament was abolished in favour of direct rule from Westminster.

The series of events culminating in the Act of Union began with Britain's involvement in the Napoleonic wars against France between 1793 and 1815. Ireland posed a serious security threat when a rebellion erupted in 1798. This was put down with considerable force and the British government decided that, to end instability in Ireland, direct rule from the Houses of Parliament in London had to be applied. For the next hundred years, Irish politics would be dominated by attempts to change or destroy that Act of Union. It would survive three rebellions – 1803, 1848 and the Fenian revolt of 1867. It would also survive economic decline in Ireland and the disaster of the Great Famine.

During the nineteenth century, Irish nationalism was represented in the British parliament by the Irish Parliamentary Party. This political group adopted a policy of disrupting the House of Commons to highlight Irish issues such as land reform and home rule. By the beginning of the twentieth century many considered this constitutional nationalism to be 'old nationalism'.

The rise of cultural nationalism in Ireland reinforced that the country had a strong cultural identity separate from Britain, which led to the belief that if the country was culturally separate then it should also be politically separate. Many organisations, including the Gaelic League and Sinn Féin, were founded in order to further Irish cultural heritage and nationalist beliefs. These organisations renewed interest in Irish history and culture among young people. They encouraged a vision of a nationalist future for Ireland and looked to past events to highlight their cause. One such event was the 1898 commemoration of the 1798 rebellion. Though the rebellion had failed, the legacy of that attempt inspired future generations to continue their quest for independence. The 1916 Rising was another such attempt.

The roots of that rebellion were fixed in the preceding years, beginning in 1911. In that year the introduction of the home rule bill for Ireland in the House of Commons was met with opposition by many unionists in Ireland. The bill offered limited independence to Ireland, but was seen as an attempt to force those who wanted to remain united with Britain into an Irish parliament. This parliament would have consisted of a House of Commons and a Senate to control domestic affairs, but with the House of Commons in London retaining the power to nullify or amend any laws.

In January 1913 the Ulster Volunteers were established by the unionist leaders Sir Edward Carson and James Craig to defend the union with Britain. In November that year the Irish Volunteers were formed to defend the ideal of home rule. Three months previously, in August 1913, leading industrialist William Martin Murphy had locked out a number of workers for their involvement in the Irish Transport and General Workers' Union (ITGWU), organised by James Larkin. The dispute escalated until it involved 400 employers and over 20,000 workers, bringing Dublin to a standstill for almost six months before hunger forced the workers, mainly unskilled labourers, to return to work. To protect workers from attacks by the police, James Connolly of the ITGWU set up a military organisation, the Irish Citizen Army, in November 1913.

As these three unofficial organisations began a campaign of military training and gun-running, the threat of civil war hung over Ireland. The outbreak of the Great War in 1914 postponed the home rule crisis which had been brewing between 1912 and 1914; but although the situation was defused, the threat still remained.[1]

The Irish Parliamentary Party was confronted with the prospect of home rule being granted after the war. At the start of the Great War membership of the Irish Volunteers was estimated at 180,000. John Redmond, the leader of the Irish Parliamentary Party, had effective control of the Irish Volunteers and encouraged many young Irishmen to join the British army as a demonstration of loyalty to the crown. The hope was that this loyalty would result in Ireland being granted home rule when the war was over.

During the following years, both nationalists and unionists swelled the ranks of the 36th Ulster division, the 16th Irish division and the 10th Irish division They were sent to France to fight side by side with British troops to repel the threat of German imperialism.

The outbreak of the war had greatly reduced the membership of the Irish Volunteers as a split had occurred. Those who joined the British army to fight in Europe became known as the National Volunteers, while those who remained at home to continue the struggle for Irish independence retained the name the Irish Volunteers; most joined the British army while only 10,000 stayed at home in the Irish Volunteers. Those who remained commenced a vigorous training regime that involved route marching, defence and attack planning, weapon training and marksmanship. The Irish Volunteers were considered a defensive force against the threat of the Ulster Volunteers. Eoin MacNeill, the leader of the Irish Volunteers, wanted to retain the organisation in an effort to deter Britain from reneging on its promise of home rule once the war was over.

However, the Irish Volunteers contained a number of radicals in its ranks and was also infiltrated by members of the Irish Republican Brotherhood (IRB). These radicals gained important executive positions within the organisation and regarded revolution as the only way to gain independence from Britain. Plans for an insurrection were drawn up by the secret military council of the IRB, which comprised Patrick Pearse, Éamonn Ceannt and Joseph Plunkett. Later they were joined by Tom Clarke and Sean McDermott. The supreme council of the Irish Volunteers, including Eoin MacNeill and Bulmer Hobson, was not informed about the uprising. Later, James Connolly was persuaded to join the Volunteers in an attempt to gain Irish independence by means of rebellion, planned for Easter 1916.[2]

A series of events in the week leading to the rebellion

was to have a dramatic effect. The secret military council decided to exploit the manoeuvres of the Irish Volunteers and issued orders to mobilise on Easter Sunday 1916; they intended to occupy a number of key positions in Dublin city and declare a republic. The military council of the IRB eventually informed MacNeill of their plan, and also that a ship named the *Aud* was making its way to Ireland from Germany, laden with arms and ammunition for the Volunteers.

MacNeill was convinced by the plan, and accepted the idea of the rebellion. However, when he heard that the *Aud* had been scuttled by her captain having been intercepted by the British navy, MacNeill withdrew his support for the rebellion, believing that any attempt was doomed to failure. To prevent the Rising from going ahead, he issued a countermanding order, cancelling all manoeuvres for Easter Sunday 1916. He relayed this information through individuals and also by an announcement published in the *Sunday Independent*. The military council, however, decided to go ahead with the rebellion and ordered its forces to assemble the next day, Easter Monday, 24 April 1916.[3]

During the mobilisation that Monday morning, it was discovered that many Volunteers had received the previous countermanding orders from MacNeill, leading to confusion within the ranks. Throughout the country small groups mobilised, but many soon stood down and returned home, unsure of the orders issued by their commanders. In Dublin, those who turned out occupied their positions and waited. It is estimated that a force of 1,500 men, women and teenage boys and girls mobilised. By the end of Easter week, that force was in direct conflict with over 20,000 trained British soldiers.

British intelligence was taken by surprise as it, too, had taken the cancellation of the manoeuvres as genuine. It had not managed to infiltrate the IRB military council and so had not received news of the mobilisation order for Monday 24 April 1916. Eoin MacNeill's decision to countermand the order was to have a detrimental effect on the Rising and especially the events that unfolded around the Mount Street Bridge area. The failure of so many to report for action on Easter Monday placed the Irish Volunteers in a precarious position, yet they carried on, believing that a failed attempt was better than no attempt at all.

2
EASTER MONDAY, 24 APRIL 1916

On the morning of Easter Monday, 24 April 1916 at 11 a.m., members of C Company, 3rd battalion of the Irish Volunteers mobilised at Earlsfort Terrace in Dublin.[4] In total only thirty-four members of the Irish Volunteers turned out as a result of Eoin MacNeill's countermanding order, leaving the battalion seriously under strength. The officers comprised the newly-promoted Simon Donnelly, who held the rank of captain, and Lieutenant Michael Malone of the Volunteers' Cyclist Corps. The group moved off in two sections, Donnelly leading the way with twenty men and Lieutenant Malone following with the remainder. Both sections made their way eastwards until they reached Upper Mount Street. Here Donnelly and Malone conferred before proceeding in different directions. Captain Donnelly led his men towards Boland's bakery, where Commandant Éamon de Valera had established his command post; de Valera had overall command of the 3rd battalion. Meanwhile, Lieutenant Malone's men continued towards Mount Street Bridge as Malone had been entrusted with holding the bridge and preventing British reinforcements from entering the city.

The original plan was to occupy five strategically located posts along the route in the locality of the bridge. The first was Carrisbrooke House at the junction of Pembroke Road and Northumberland Road, from where the field of fire would cover Ballsbridge and the approach to the city. The second position was 25 Northumberland Road, which would cover Northumberland Road and the main gate of Beggars Bush barracks. The third and fourth positions were the parochial hall and the schoolhouse, which would provide covering fire for the men in 25 Northumberland Road. Clanwilliam House, the fifth position, would cover Mount Street Bridge, Northumberland Road and the canal bank. Later, a sixth position would be occupied – Robert's building yard, fronting Clanwilliam Place to Lower Grand Canal Street.

With Carrisbrooke House to be occupied by Volunteers from another unit, Lieutenant Malone dispersed his own men as follows: Section Commander James Grace and two Volunteers, Paddy Byrne and Michael Rowe, took up position in 25 Northumberland Road – the residents of number 25 had vacated their house as they were sympathetic to the Volunteers and had been forewarned of the occupation. The parochial hall farther along Northumberland Road was occupied by Section Commander Patrick Doyle and three other Volunteers – Joseph Clarke, James McGrath and William Christian. An employee of the Sinn Féin Bank, Joe Clarke had been a Volunteer since the successful Howth gun-running of 1914. The schoolhouse on the opposite side of the road held four Volunteers, Adjutant Denis O' Donoghue, James Kavanagh, Robert Cooper and James Doyle.

The final position in the original plan was Clanwilliam House, a large three-storey Georgian building with long sash windows that commanded an excellent view of Mount Street Bridge and the other positions held by the Volunteers.[5] This position was occupied by Section Commander George Reynolds (who had one arm in a sling due to blood poisoning). A fluent Gaelic and French speaker, Reynolds was also a talented ecclesiastical silversmith. He was accompanied by Volunteers Daniel Byrne, William Ronan and James Doyle, while another younger Volunteer joined them soon after. When the Volunteers entered the house, they moved its occupants, Miss Wilson and her mother, into the dining-room.

Reynolds soon discarded the sling as he ordered his men to their positions. The Volunteers secured their positions by barricading the doors and windows with the furniture that was to hand. Coal was taken from the basement and wrapped in sheets. These were used to barricade the windows and were then covered with blankets.[6] Later in the day Reynolds suggested to Miss Wilson that she should collect her valuables and secure them in a back room of the house; he locked the door of this room and gave Miss Wilson the key. Clanwilliam House was considered a keep and the last line of defence in the Volunteers' efforts to prevent British troops from entering the city. This building was to be held at all costs.

The Volunteers were armed with a variety of weapons, including Lee Enfield, Martini Henry and Mauser rifles from the Howth landing and an assortment of revolvers and automatic pistols. Lieutenant Malone carried a Mauser automatic pistol, a formidable weapon that could be fitted with a shoulder stock, thus transforming the gun into a carbine. It was lent to Malone by his commanding officer, Éamon de Valera. The weapon was nicknamed 'Peter the Painter' after the anarchist Peter Piatkov. Using this formidable weapon, Malone wreaked havoc among the tightly packed ranks of British troops during the engagement.

Malone was twenty-eight years old and a devoted member of the St Patrick's Confraternity in Ringsend. He was a carpenter by profession and had distinguished himself in the technical schools where he had won many prizes for drawing and carving. His appointment as lieutenant reflected his excellent leadership skills and also his ability to handle a weapon, as he was deemed a master marksman. Less than a year earlier, on 24 May 1915, his brother, William Malone, had been killed in action in France serving as a sergeant with the 2nd battalion of the Royal Dublin Fusiliers. Lieutenant Michael Malone was the last Volunteer to take up position at 25 Northumberland Road.[7]

At 4 p.m. the first shots of the impending battle were fired. At Clanwilliam House, George Reynolds looked through his field glasses and saw a number of khaki-clad figures lying motionless near the junction of Haddington Road and Northumberland Road. The figures were members of the veteran defence force known as the 'Georgius Rex' or, as they had been humorously christened by Dubliners, 'The Gorgeous Wrecks'. These men, most of them veteran soldiers, had been on manoeuvre near Kingstown (now Dún Laoghaire). Though they carried weapons, they had no ammunition. The force consisted of 120 men and officers. They were returning to barracks when they heard news of the rebellion in the city. Nearing their destination the column split into two sections. The main body, led by Major Harris of the Trinity College officer training corps, turned right along Shelbourne Road, where they came under fire from Volunteers who had been despatched from Boland's bakery and had taken up position on the railway embankment.

The British force made a dash for the barracks and

many succeeded in entering the main gate, taking with them a Corporal Clery who had been mortally wounded. Others from that section ran up Lansdowne Road and scaled the wall into the barracks grounds. They found the barracks in a state of confusion as soldiers there only had seventeen Lee Enfield rifles to defend the building with. The extra six Enfields that the veterans were carrying were most welcome. The others were advised to use their Italian rifles as clubs in the event of an assault on the barracks. In total, eighty-one men and nine officers survived the initial shots fired from the embankment. The second section of the veteran defence force, forty men under the command of F.H. Browning, had forked left as they neared the barracks and marched along Northumberland Road.

The sound of gunfire suddenly echoed throughout the street as the veterans reached Lieutenant Malone's position. Local residents gazed in horror as many of the veterans fell, either dead or wounded. The first to be hit was shot through the head, blood streaming from the wound. The veterans took cover behind trees and behind the steps that led to the front doors of the houses in the area. Four men were killed, including Browning, and nine wounded. Passers-by rushed to their aid; the injured were taken to local houses where their wounds were dressed. F.H. Browning was president of the Irish Rugby Union and one of Ireland's outstanding cricketers.[8] Malone and Grace held their fire when they realised the veterans were not carrying any ammunition. The Georgius Rex then made their way rapidly to Beggars Bush barracks; they immediately took up positions on the roof and began firing at number 25 and also at the Volunteers on the railway embankment.

One of the garrison at the barracks made his way over the wall and proceeded to 28 Northumberland Road, where he opened fire on Malone's position. It took some time to determine this sniper's exact location, but when Section Commander Grace heard the report of Malone's pistol, he saw the sniper in the house opposite clutch at the window blind as he was hit, before falling to the floor, dead.

Lieutenant John Guilfoyle of A Company of the Irish Volunteers had left Boland's bakery and occupied a position in the cottages across from the main gate of Beggars Bush barracks. His continuous firing from the cottages harassed the garrison and restricted their movements.

The firing stopped soon after and an uneasy calm descended on the area. The rifles that lay in the street were collected by some young boys, who then handed them over to the Irish Volunteers at the parochial hall. News of this skirmish provoked anger throughout the city and condemnation from the public as the veterans were deemed to be unarmed as they carried no ammunition. Patrick Pearse, commander-in-chief of the Irish Volunteers, issued an order to his men forbidding any Volunteer to fire on an unarmed man, whether in uniform or not.

It was at this point that Lieutenant Malone decided to send Paddy Byrne and Michael Rowe home as he believed they were too young to become engaged in the action he knew was inevitable. Having released the two Volunteers from their duty, Malone and Grace positioned themselves in number 25 and found vantage points that gave them a commanding view of Northumberland Road and Haddington Road. This left only two men in C Company's most advanced outpost. Leaving Clanwilliam House, Section Leader George Reynolds then made a sortie to Malone's position; while passing the schoolhouse he conversed with Company Adjutant Denis O'Donoghue about the firing farther down the road. Both agreed that their orders were to stop any attempt to enter the city, by those dressed in khaki or otherwise.

On returning to Clanwilliam House, Reynolds sent home the youngest member of his contingent as he had begun to show signs of nerves. The Volunteers rested for the night, with only James Doyle managing to get some sleep. Reynolds remained awake. Pickets were placed at all their positions and the Volunteers remained vigilant, ready for any impending attack.

British High Command in Ireland issued a request for reinforcements from England in order to suppress the rebellion. At 7.30 p.m. on Monday, 24 April, the 59th North Midland division, under the command of Major General A.E. Sandbach, received orders to mobilise. The division consisted of three brigades: the 176th (2/5th, 2/6th, South Staffordshire regiment, 2/5th, 2/6th North Staffordshire regiment); 177th (2/4th, 2/5th Lincolnshire regiment, 2/4th, 2/5th Leicestershire regiment) and 178th infantry division (2/5th, 2/6th, 2/7th and 2/8th battalions of the Sherwood Forester regiment). All leave was cancelled and officers returned to barracks. The troops prepared to move out.

3

TUESDAY, 25 APRIL 1916

At daybreak on Tuesday, 25 April, Section Commander George Reynolds, in position at Clanwilliam House, sent James Doyle to the schoolhouse to ask Adjutant Denis O'Donoghue if he could exchange some 303 mark VII ammunition for mark VI, as the larger calibre was not suitable for Martini Henry rifles. On reaching the position Doyle discovered that the schoolhouse had been vacated, leaving the Volunteers' flank exposed. Arriving back at Clanwilliam House he found Reynolds in conversation with Lieutenant Malone. The school garrison had been moved to Boland's bakery. Both men agreed that their positions needed strengthening and Malone suggested that Reynolds should send to Boland's bakery for food and reinforcements.

The battalion was seriously under strength as many men had failed to turn out due to the countermanding order issued by MacNeill. The 3rd battalion effectively controlled troop movements from Beggars Bush barracks.

Reynolds despatched Daniel Byrne to Boland's bakery with a request for supplies and men. He soon returned with an ample supply of fruit cakes and loaves of bread but no reinforcements. Reynolds sent Byrne back to the bakery and this time he met Captain Simon Donnelly, the officer commanding C Company. Donnelly sent Richard Murphy, Patrick Doyle, and Thomas and James Walsh (brothers) to reinforce the position at Clanwilliam House.[9] Murphy was a tailor by trade and due to get married in Easter week. Doyle was deeply religious and attended mass every day in Milltown church. His talents within the battalion lay in his expertise as a musketry instructor. Captain Donnelly sent Daniel Byrne elsewhere with despatches. The garrison at Clanwilliam House now numbered seven men.

Shots rang out near the bridge. A car occupied by a British royal army medical corps (RAMC) officer and a civilian had attempted to drive past the occupied positions and was met with firing from the Volunteers at Grand Canal Street and Clanwilliam House. The civilian, Richard Waters from Monkstown, was badly wounded and taken from the scene in a milk-car; he died later. The RAMC officer, a Captain Scovell, escaped uninjured. Both men were unarmed and were not challenged to stop.

At 11 a.m. Lieutenant Malone made his way to Clanwilliam House to check on the situation. He found the men in good spirits and agreed to Reynolds' suggestion that the owners of the house, the Wilsons, should be sent away as it would be a tragedy if they were harmed in any way. When the Wilsons left, the men in Clanwilliam House set about re-fortifying their position – barricading the ground floor with large wardrobes and choosing the large drawing-room as the best vantage point for the forthcoming action. Mattresses were laid on the floor and ammunition placed near the windows. Vessels were filled with water and sheets were torn for bandages. Reynolds, Dick Murphy and Patrick Doyle investigated a trapdoor on the top landing that offered the Volunteers a means of escape if the building was stormed. When everything possible had been done, the Volunteers took up their positions and waited.

After all these preparations, Tuesday passed with few distractions. Local women appeared in the courtyards shouting abuse at the Volunteers, but Reynolds ordered his men to remain calm. A local man brought news that the fighting around St Stephen's Green was heavy and that British troops had taken over the Shelbourne hotel. Reynolds posted a lookout in case an attack came from the city side of the bridge. That night the silence was broken by gunfire that echoed throughout the city. The reports of the Volunteers' Mauser rifles were very different from those of the British army's Enfields, and so the two could be easily distinguished.

Many of the 59th division, and especially the Sherwood Forester regiments, were in training at Watford. These men, from places such as Newark, Mansfield, Radford and Alfreton, were volunteers who had left behind the midland industries of lace, leather and tobacco manufacturing. Others worked in agriculture or the law, or as clerks and shop assistants. With only six weeks of basic training completed, they believed they were on their way to the Western Front. Many had not completed their musketry training as the initial training – involving square bashing and filling sandbags – was in preparation for war in Belgium and France. The 59th division was ill-prepared for mobilisation as officers and ordinary ranks were on leave. Messages stating that all 178th brigade men were to return to their billets immediately were flashed across cinema screens. Some men had been out on special duties in relation to German Zeppelin raids and when they returned to barracks they were given the immediate order to fall in and prepare to move out.

The first trains left Watford at 4 a.m. and others followed at 8.30 a.m. and 10.00 a.m. As the trains moved northwards some of the men thought they were destined for Russia.

Troops were issued with 120 rounds of ammunition, field dressings and iodine ampoules. At this point, however, their final destination remained unknown to them, although some officers had purchased newspapers that related the story of an attempted landing of arms and ammunition on the coast of Ireland.

On Monday evening, 24 April, the following announcement was made by the press bureau:

> The Secretary of the Admiralty announces. During the period p.m. 20 April and p.m. 21 April an attempt to land arms and ammunition was made by a vessel under the guise of a neutral merchant ship, but in reality a German auxiliary, in conjunction with a German submarine. The auxiliary sank and a number of prisoners were made, amongst whom was Sir Roger Casement.[10]

Many now guessed they were heading to Ireland. On reaching Liverpool, officers who had been briefed tried to acquire maps of Dublin from local hotels and guesthouses. However, many experienced officers were ordered to stay behind, and this had a detrimental affect on the Sherwood Forester regiment. The logistical problems of moving four battalions from Liverpool to Dublin soon became apparent. Troops assembled at the Prince's landing stage. The first three companies left on the SS *Patriotic* at 8 p.m., while others left on the SS *Tynwald*. HMS *Oscia* escorted the Nottingham and Derbyshire regiments to Kingstown

(Dún Laoghaire), with men of the Staffordshire regiment also on board. Brigadier Colonel Ernest William Stuart King Maconchy and his staff, as well as some men of the battalion, had left at 3.30 p.m. on the mail ship *The Ulster* which had been taken from its usual run to Holyhead. Though the first troops began arriving in Dublin at 10 o'clock that evening, it was 5.30 the following morning before all the troops were assembled at Kingstown. During this embarkation process an event that greatly assisted the Irish Volunteers occurred. Each battalion had been equipped with two Lewis machine guns. This drum-fed weapon, capable of firing up to 550 rounds per minute, was a formidable infantry support weapon.

However, the embarkation officer on the quayside instructed that the Lewis machine guns were to remain behind and reiterated that the message received from Ireland was 'that men were wanted and not guns'. Loud protests were made, but to no avail. The failure to bring this support weapon was to prove costly. The only weapons the troops had were rifles and bayonets. They had very little experience in using either, and their lack of training, both for the Western Front and a new type of urban warfare in Dublin, was to cost the regiment dearly.

Lieutenant Colonel W. Coape Oates of the 2/8th Sherwood Forester regiment wrote of the military red tape that greeted the men:

… the British army seems fated to have its work blocked or rendered as difficult as possible by officials dressed with a little brief authority, whose orders may not be questioned, and who rarely have to answer for after results.[11]

4
WEDNESDAY, 26 APRIL 1916 MORNING

As British troops disembarked at Kingstown, many of the men thought they were in France and some even greeted the local girls with 'bonjour ma'moiselle'. However, they soon learned that a rebellion had broken out in Dublin, with many key positions held by rebels, and that an attempt would be made to keep crown forces from entering the city. Food was in short supply as the kitchens and transports had not yet arrived. Men devoured their rations and bought sandwiches from locals, who quickly set up stalls. The 2/5th and 2/6th fared better, treated to bacon and eggs as they rested in the grounds of a local school outside the town, while officers were given breakfast at the local yacht club, where they soon learned of the events of the last forty-eight hours.

The 178th infantry brigade was under the overall command of Brigadier Colonel Maconchy, and he summoned his commanding officers at 8.30 a.m. to give them their orders:

(1) The rebels are preparing to oppose troop movements from Kingstown to Dublin.

(2) Troops will therefore advance in two parallel columns; the left, consisting of the 2/5th and 2/6th Sherwood Foresters (Derbyshire troops), will advance inland along the Stillorgan–Donnybrook route; the right, comprising 2/7th and 2/8th (Nottingham), will follow the coast road through Ballsbridge. Destination in both cases will be the Royal Hospital, Kilmainham (British military headquarters in Ireland). Starting point Kingstown Harbour 10.30 a.m.

(3) The right column will be led by the Robin Hoods (the 2/7th) order of companies: first C Company (Captain F. Pragnell), second A (Captain H.C. Wright), three B (Major H. Hanson) and four D (Captain L.L. Cooper). OC advance guard will dispose his platoons as follows: one in advance, one to clear houses overlooking the road, one to deal with side roads, one in support. Every house and side road will be searched and cleared.

(4) Fall in: 10.15 a.m.[12]

The Staffordshire brigade under the command of Brigadier General Carlton was to remain in reserve at Kingstown.

As many of the men had less than three months' service, Lieutenant Colonel W. Coape Oates, who was in command of the 2/8th Sherwood Foresters, ordered his men down to the quayside. This experienced officer had served with the Royal Munster Fusiliers and knew the danger of having inexperienced men thrown into combat. The soldiers were ordered to load, present and fire out into the sea in order to become familiar with their weapons.

The troops moved off. The commanding officer, Lieutenant Colonel Cecil Fane, went forward with the advance guard and Major Rayner marched at the head of the main body. The two groups were connected by Lieutenant Hewitt, who commanded a party of scouts, and information was relayed at regular intervals. The men were surprised at their reception when they reached the suburbs of the city – they marched to the sound of cheering crowds and refreshments were pressed upon them. A significant number of the local women had husbands and sons fighting for the cause of small nations in France and Belgium, and the disruption caused by the Irish Volunteers meant that many had not received their army pension payments. They welcomed the British soldiers as liberators who would restore law and order to Ireland.

Captain Frederick Dietrichsen was adjutant of the 2/7th Sherwood Forester regiment and had previously been a barrister in Nottingham before joining up. As he marched through the streets he was surprised and delighted to see his wife Beatrice and their two children aged three and seven standing on the pavement waving to him. He had sent his family to Ireland to protect them from the ever-increasing German Zeppelin raids. His wife Beatrice was originally from Blackrock in Dublin and was staying with her parents there. Captain Dietrichsen dropped out of formation and hugged his family at the side of the road. He was to be one of the first killed in action during the battle of Mount Street.

Across the city, Richard Sheane from Wicklow made his way to the Royal Dublin Society (RDS) in Ballsbridge to attend his stall at the spring show. He witnessed the advance guard of the Sherwood Forester regiment as they reached Ballsbridge at about 11.50 a.m.:

> The poor chaps were almost completely done up by their tramp along the hard road from Kingstown, under a blazing sun, and carrying their ninety pound kit. After about ten minutes' rest, the detachment moved off citywards and as the main body had now come up, there was a column of troops as far as we could see, in the direction of Kingstown.[13]

They halted for a short rest at the front of the building. Refreshments were given to the troops by onlookers attending the spring show and valuable information in relation to the local situation was gathered. Their information was that many of the rebels were dressed in green uniforms and suggested that Northumberland Road was likely to prove dangerous.

Brigadier General L.B. Carlton of the 177th brigade

and Brigadier Colonel Maconchy (originally from Longford) of the 178th brigade set up their headquarters in the Pembroke town hall at Ballsbridge. Lieutenants Colonel Oates and Fane were summoned and the order was given to take the schoolhouse just south of Mount Street Bridge on the Grand Canal. This was a strong point known to be occupied by the rebels and was likely to prove troublesome. Once this had been taken, the officer commanding the 2/8th was to bring up his battalion, which consisted of three companies (A, B, C), pass through the area secured by the 2/7th and penetrate as far as possible in the direction of Trinity College.

As Tuesday morning dawned the garrison at Clanwilliam House could hear the distant rumble of artillery fire and the crack of musketry coming from the direction of the city centre. The men were restless, having held the position for almost forty-eight hours with only a slight skirmish with the enemy to break the monotony. They had made themselves comfortable, using the large drawing-room as a place to sit. Food arrived for Thomas and James Walsh via their younger brother. However, as the bottom level of the house was barricaded, getting the food into the house proved awkward, but was soon achieved. Tom Walsh had just drawn up the parcel of food on some string when a man cycled past and declared that the British had landed at Kingstown and were heading in this direction.[14]

Reynolds ordered the men to their posts and to fix the sights on their rifles at 300 yards; they knelt and prayed before taking up their positions. In the drawing room there were three windows. Patrick Doyle and Dick Murphy occupied the window on the right, Reynolds took the window in the middle and Jimmy Doyle and Willie Ronan took up position at the left window. Tom Walsh and his brother took their positions at the side and rear windows. Boxes of ammunition lay open beside each post. Tom opened his food parcel and, realising that this might be the garrison's last supper, decided to share it with his comrades. The parcel was placed on the drawing-room table and they all ate quietly, their minds preoccupied with the task ahead.[15]

The four Volunteers in the parochial hall had also been waiting patiently for some form of action. Their position was not in line with the other buildings on the road as the hall stood a good distance from the footpath. Though it was harder to see what was approaching their location, they were well placed to deal with any attempt to pass the hall. The men were adequately armed and the parochial hall, like the other outposts, was well fortified against a frontal assault.

At 25 Northumberland Road, Lieutenant Michael Malone and Section Commander James Grace waited for action. James Grace's sister, Bridget, along with May Cullen, arrived at the house. These two women were members of Cumann na mBan, the women's division of the Irish Volunteers. They knocked on the front door but James Grace explained that they could not be admitted as the door had been barricaded. The women announced that they had food and a despatch from James Connolly with them. Grace told them to place the despatch in the letter-box but that they would have to do without the food. The despatch warned the men that British reinforcements had landed at Kingstown and were advancing towards the city centre. If they proceeded towards the city via Northumberland Road, they were to be stopped.

Lieutenant Malone considered changing their post to Carrisbrooke House, at the junction of Northumberland Road and Pembroke Road. Malone, who had reconnoitred the area on Tuesday night, had discovered that this important post had been vacated. The Volunteers from the Blackrock company had taken up sniping positions in the surrounding area. The decision to vacate this station had left the entire 3rd battalion at Boland's bakery in danger of being outflanked. If the advancing British troops turned left they would carry on down Pembroke Road towards Baggot Street Bridge and onwards to St Stephen's Green. If they marched right they would be on Northumberland Road and heading towards Mount Street Bridge. As the Volunteers prepared to move their post, Malone spied, through his binoculars, the advancing Sherwood Foresters. The British soldiers advanced cautiously with fixed bayonets. He could see clearly the strain on their young faces. Malone abandoned the idea of moving their position and the Irish Volunteers took up their posts at the windows of 25 Northumberland Road. The waiting was almost over.

5

WEDNESDAY, 26 APRIL 1916 EARLY AFTERNOON

Richard Sheane saw the first action involving the Sherwood Forester regiment from his position at the railings
of the RDS:

> Just as the head of the column reached about the centre of
> the bridge, they were met by a volley of fire from the house in
> front of them, and about two hundred yards distant from the
> place where we were standing. One man fell on the bridge
> and this appeared to be the only casualty.
>
> As the snipers continued to fire on them the troops got
> orders to take cover. A firing party ran forward, and lying
> about three feet apart in a line across the roadway, com-
> menced firing on their attackers.[16]

This incident occurred as the regiment crossed the Dodder river in Ballsbridge at about 12.15 p.m. The shots had

been fired from the vicinity of Carrisbrooke House. As the Sherwood Forester regiment opened fire on the building, the Volunteers moved position and took to sniping in the surrounding area. The British soldiers stormed the house without further hindrance and then paused to assess the situation.

The 2/7th Sherwood Foresters then advanced along Northumberland Road. The main body halted at St Mary's Road under the command of Major Rayner. A reconnaissance platoon, commanded by Lieutenant William Foster, was sent out to check the right flank of the advancing Sherwood Foresters as intelligence had revealed that the Irish Volunteers were entrenched along the railway line.

C Company moved forward, led by Lieutenant Colonel Cecil Fane, Captain Frank Pragnell and the Adjutant, Captain Frederick Dietrichsen. As they reached the junction of Northumberland Road and Haddington Road they came under intense fire from Lieutenant Malone's position at 25 Northumberland Road. The first volley of shots claimed ten British soldiers, among them Captain Dietrichsen.

The order to 'drop' was yelled by Captain Pragnell and the inexperienced British soldiers lay down in the roadway and took up firing positions. Many were wounded as they lay prone in the street in full view of Lieutenant Malone's and Grace's weapons. The building housing the Volunteers was identified by Captain Pragnell, who ordered his men to open fire. The soldiers fired a volley at the building. The British officers then drew their swords and, shouting 'charge', raced towards the front entrance of Malone's position. As they reached the steps of the house the soldiers were caught by intense fire from not only 25 Northumberland Road but also the garrison at Clanwilliam House. They could not access the house as the ground floor entrance was well barricaded. Fane and Pragnell could not identify where the main body of fire was coming from and took cover by the railings. Fane decided to outflank the Volunteers at number 25 by sending Major Hanson and B Company up Haddington Road to secure Baggot Street Bridge and then move back towards Mount Street Bridge via the canal bank.

As Major Hanson and B Company moved off, the other Sherwood Foresters lay down a covering fire against 25, 26, 27 and 28 Northumberland Road. However, as the troops moved around the house, a devastating fire was trained on them from a side window, and the first section of Major Hanson's men suffered heavy casualties from Malone's automatic pistol. Nonetheless, Hanson pressed on and succeeded in passing the house and moving off towards Baggot Street Bridge. His section had lost many men – this type of warfare was very different than that for which they had been training.

Colonel Fane was wounded by a bullet that shattered his left arm. He dismissed the stretcher-bearers that came to his aid, handed over his command to Major Rayner and then staggered back to the houses along Northumberland Road where he had his wound dressed at an improvised dressing station.

Inside 25 Northumberland Road, Lieutenant Malone and James Grace took careful aim as the Sherwood Foresters approached. The advancing British soldiers buckled under the first enfilade and many dropped to the ground, writhing in agony. The shots, however, did not disperse the soldiers and they took up positions on the roadway. Malone and Grace had positioned themselves strategically on the upper floors of number 25, thus giving them the advantage of height over their attackers. They inflicted many fatalities as they fired down into the ranks of the exposed British troops, who had failed to take adequate cover.

As the Irish Volunteers paused to reload, the Sherwood Foresters charged the house but were repulsed by gunfire from the Volunteers at the parochial hall and Clanwilliam House. An attempt by the British to outflank the house was unsuccessful, as Malone had positioned himself at the bathroom window at the side of the house. This vantage point gave a commanding view of both Northumberland Road and Haddington Road.

The Volunteers at Clanwilliam House heard the crack of rifle fire as the advancing British troops were halted at Northumberland Road. They now released the safety catches of their weapons, drew the bolts back and released bullets into the breeches. As the British soldiers attempted to storm Malone's position the contingent at Clanwilliam House unleashed a fusillade into the ranks of the charging Sherwood Foresters. George Reynolds could be heard cheering Malone with the words 'good old Mick'.

Colonel Fane resumed command of his company of Foresters as soon as his arm had been dressed. Lieutenant Foster returned from his reconnaissance, confirming that the Volunteers were entrenched on the railway line. He and his men took cover in the gardens of the houses and laid down a covering fire against number 25. However, as the Sherwood Foresters attempted to pass Malone's position they encountered heavy and direct fire as Malone and Grace continued to inflict severe losses on the British soldiers.

Major Hanson and the men of B Company succeeded in reaching Baggot Street Bridge. Here he posted a platoon to guard the bridge and then moved back towards the fighting via the canal bank and Percy Place. His objective was to capture the schoolhouse, which he believed was occupied by the Volunteers. As Hanson and his men drew near to the building they tried to gain entry to one of the nearby houses but came under concentrated fire from the Walsh brothers at Clanwilliam House. The Foresters raced for cover, some crouching behind the canal bank walls. Hanson could not determine where the shots had come from and thought his section had been fired upon from the houses they were trying to enter. The soldiers opened fire on these buildings and then charged up the steps, yelling to give themselves courage and to vent their frustration. On entering one of the houses they found a terrified Miss Scully and her maid and placed them under arrest.

At Clanwilliam House the Walsh brothers, who had the side and rear entrances covered, saw Hanson and his section advance along the canal bank towards the schoolhouse. These two men had not yet fired at the British soldiers as their position did not face out onto Northumberland Road. Tom Walsh took aim at the crouching khaki figures. This time, as the Mauser rifle fired, the recoil of the weapon knocked him unconscious. It took him a few minutes to regain consciousness. His brother, Jim, opened fire as the Sherwood Foresters attempted to gain entrance to the front door of a house along the canal bank. Several soldiers tumbled over. Both brothers then began firing into the ranks of the Foresters, pinning them down and inflicting heavy losses.[17]

A whistle sounded and a large number of soldiers charged down Northumberland Road. Some raced up the steps of number 25 only to be repelled by Malone and Grace. Others ran past that position towards the schoolhouse. As they came abreast of the parochial hall the Volunteers within opened fire and many soldiers fell severely wounded in the street. That post had still not been identified by the British as being occupied by the Volunteers. Those that managed to get past the hall were met by a volley of fire from the Volunteers in Clanwilliam House. Of the sixty Sherwood Foresters that began the charge less than twelve reached the schoolhouse.

The soldiers who came onto the bridge were met by more gunfire as the men at Clanwilliam House took up their revolvers and emptied their contents at the remaining British soldiers. The scene was one of utter carnage. Death and destruction covered the length of the road. Many of the wounded took cover, bewildered and confused as to where the shooting was coming from. An officer, Lieutenant Percy Claude Perry, lay dead on the approach to the bridge. The wounded who lay in the street moved to take off their heavy equipment. They took water bottles from their pouches and drank greedily, many succumbing to the heat and exhaustion of battle.

At this stage Captain Simon Donnelly, who was in Boland's bakery, despatched three men and accompanied them to Roberts' yard, which adjoined Clanwilliam Terrace. Simon Donnelly later named two of the men – Seamus Kavanagh of C Company and Seamus Doyle of the 1st battalion.[18] He did not remember the name of the third Volunteer but in all probability it was Adjutant Denis O'Donoghue, who had originally held the position at the schoolhouse. These men took up their positions in the yard, bringing the total number of Volunteers at the battle to seventeen.

At Clanwilliam House George Reynolds gave his orders: 'If they charge again, the two men in the right window are to fire to the left side of the road, the two in the left window are to fire to the right side of the road. I will take the middle of the road.'

This ensured that the width of Northumberland Road and Mount Street Bridge were covered and that any attempt to break through would be fatal. He also told the Walsh brothers that it was vital to try and clear Percy Place of British soldiers as this was the escape route for the Volunteers at 25 Northumberland Road and also for those in the parochial hall.

Major Hanson and his men had been pinned down along the canal bank and had suffered many fatalities. Hanson himself had been wounded, as had Second Lieutenant Lamb and Second Lieutenant Hartshorn. What remained of B Company had taken cover behind the low walls that bordered the canal. The Walsh brothers at Clanwilliam House fired at the crouching British soldiers as they came into sight through the breaks in the walls. They were quite conspicuous because their large haversacks gave away their positions. In an attempt to break out of their situation, Company Sergeant Major Towlson proceeded to move out onto the bridge. Simon Donnelly and the Volunteers at Roberts' yard opened fire on the

British soldiers and as they scrambled back to cover they realised that they were now hemmed in with Volunteers on both sides of the canal bank.

At Clanwilliam House Tom Walsh ceased firing as his weapon overheated. He could hear his brother Jim firing in the room above and decided to move upstairs and recommend that they both clean their weapons to avoid a possible jamming. Using a ramrod they both cleaned their rifles, getting rid of the residue that had built up from continuous firing.

As Tom Walsh moved to the room downstairs and resumed his position he noticed three bullet holes in the shutter where his head would have been. Examining these holes he was perplexed by the angle that they took. He soon realised that they had been fired from the church spire of St Mary's church on Haddington Road and brought this to the attention of George Reynolds.[19] The question of whether the Volunteers could fire on the church crossed his mind – as they were all devout Catholics – but they continued the fight.

Colonel Fane then made another attempt to outflank the Volunteers who, he believed, still held the schoolhouse. He ordered Captain H.C. Wright and A Company to move towards Grand Canal Street via Beggars Bush barracks and then proceed back along the canal bank. As Wright moved past the barracks the officer commanding, Colonel Frederick Shaw, took some of the Sherwood

Foresters to reinforce the garrison there. This left Wright with fewer men and, as they reached Grand Canal Street, they attempted to move some barricades that had been set up by Captain Donnelly and the Irish Volunteers at Boland's bakery. The British soldiers had almost stumbled upon Éamon de Valera's position. The Volunteers at Roberts' yard opened fire, as did Joseph Guilfoyle, who had positioned himself on a tower located in the railway yards. The Sherwood Foresters broke formation and retreated in disorder. Captain Wright managed to regroup his men but, rather than proceed onwards, he halted his force and decided to contact Colonel Fane for further orders. Another attempt to break through had been stopped.

The garrison holding Beggars Bush barracks were being constantly sniped at from the Volunteers positioned on the railway bridge at South Lotts Road. Sir Frederick Shaw, the officer commanding the barracks, ordered Captain E. Gerrard of the royal field artillery to lead a sortie out of the barracks to remove the enemy from their position on the nearby railway bridge. He was to take some of the newly arrived Sherwood Foresters. Gerrard described them as follows: 'They were untrained, undersized products of the English slums ... The young Sherwoods I had with me had never fired a service rifle before. They were not even able to load them. We had to show them how to load them.'[20]

Colour Quarter Master Sergeant Gamble of the Royal

Irish regiment was shot dead and Captain Gerrard was severely wounded in the arm as they attempted to dislodge the Volunteers from the railway bridge. They retreated back to the barracks.

The sermon preached in the garrison chapel that day advised the congregation to 'Keep your heads down and your hearts up.'

6

By 2.45 p.m. Colonel Fane contacted brigade headquarters. He reported that the situation was proving desperate and that the regiment had taken Baggot Street Bridge but was held up at Northumberland Road and also at Mount Street Bridge, where they had suffered many casualties. To achieve his objective he told brigade that he urgently needed machine guns and bombs. Irish command suggested contacting Captain Jeffares of the Elm Park Bombing School of Instruction, near Ballsbridge. Captain Jeffares arrived later in the afternoon with an ample supply of guncotton and Mills hand grenades. These explosives eventually turned the tide of battle.

Colonel Fane called up the 2/7th reserve D Company under the command of Captain L.L. Cooper. They were told to occupy some of the houses near the junction of Northumberland Road and Haddington Road and to prepare to lay down covering fire against 25 Northumberland Road. Captain Pragnell was ordered to take C Company, pass 25 Northumberland Road via Haddington Road, proceed to Baggot Street and then move back along the canal bank and reinforce Major Hanson's unit and attempt to secure the bridge. This involved running the gauntlet of Lieutenant Michael Malone's position once again.

The Sherwood Foresters opened fire on number 25 and as Captain Pragnell and his company raced past Malone's position they were met by a hail of bullets. Once again Malone inflicted heavy casualties on the British as Pragnell lost ten men to Malone's deadly marksmanship. It was here that Lieutenant William Victor Hawken was killed. Pragnell had succeeded in passing number 25, however, and continued on towards his destination.

Those inside 25 Northumberland Road felt the whole house shudder as the Sherwood Foresters opened fire and the bullets tore into the wood and plasterwork. James Grace was later to state that all he could do was keep his head down and 'tremble from head to foot in a panic of fear'. He felt for the first time the desperate feeling of being trapped and could only occasionally lift his head to aim and fire back. Malone continued to fire from the side window and watched as the soldiers racing by clutched at their bodies, threw their arms upwards and fell on the road as his bullets found their mark.

At the parochial hall the Volunteers still held their position. The Sherwood Foresters who attempted to pass this post were enfiladed and pinned down. The British still looked to the schoolhouse as their main objective and were unaware that the Volunteers were shooting at them from the hall. As each British wave came charging down Northumberland Road they received a devastating broadside from the Volunteers holding the hall. The failure to identify this position at an early stage only added to their mounting losses.

The Volunteers at Clanwilliam House kept up a devastating rate of fire as they surveyed the environs of their position. For over an hour no attempt had been made by the British to attack and an uneasy calm lay over the area. Tom and Jim Walsh moved towards the front room where the other Volunteers were in position. George Reynolds was kneeling at the middle window and motioned for them to come closer. As they all looked out the window they were astonished to see that the street was teeming with khaki-clad troops. The author Max Caulfield has described the scene the Volunteers witnessed from Clanwilliam House:

There were Khaki troops everywhere – crouched behind flights of front steps, behind the garden hedges, behind the trees lining Northumberland Road. And lying in the road, especially lying in the road. Four great Khaki caterpillars pulsated towards them like obscene monsters. Two lines had stretched themselves in the gutters and two more crawled along on their bellies, jammed against the coping stones. It was not like killing men; it was more like trying to slaughter a great insect or animal.[21]

The Walshes returned to their positions and started firing again. Every few minutes a whistle was sounded and British troops charged up Northumberland Road in an attempt to take the bridge. None of them ever reached the halfway mark as bullets from number 25, the parochial hall, Clanwilliam House and Roberts' yard repeatedly found their mark. However, the Volunteers soon heard the sound of explosions as British troops used hand grenades while attempting to storm Malone's position. Once again they were beaten back by Malone's and Grace's fire.

The street was covered in British dead and wounded, whose moans filled the air. Captain Arthur Dickson, who later commanded a firing squad on 8 May 1916 at Kilmainham gaol, advanced along Northumberland Road with a number of men. Bullets chipped the pavement and gateposts as they sought cover behind the trees that lined the kerbside. It was only afterwards that he realised that a ricochet had hit the pavement and lodged in his field service pocket notebook, saving his life. Later he felt a sense of guilt as he reflected on this unusual twist of fate that saved him while so many of his friends were killed in action.

As the gun smoke cleared, both the British troops and the Irish Volunteers were greeted by a most unusual spectacle. Two young women appeared on the bridge carrying large jugs of water and began administering its contents to the wounded British soldiers. They were followed by two doctors dressed in white coats, with their hands raised above their heads. The women sought permission from George Reynolds at Clanwilliam House to attend to the wounded. Reynolds nodded his approval and the firing from Clanwilliam House ceased, followed a short time later by that of the British army. Nurses followed the doctors as they tended the wounded.

The events that led to this strange ceasefire had begun a short while earlier. Having witnessed the carnage at Mount Street Bridge, Mr Redmond Howard and a local methodist minister, Reverend Hall from Dalkey, had proceeded down the laneway at the back of Clanwilliam House and made their way to Sir Patrick Dun's hospital. There they found a number of doctors and nurses waiting in the doorway deliberating on the best way to lend assistance to the wounded. Dr Myles Keogh and Dr C.B. O'Brien, two well-known practitioners, were among those waiting. Redmond Howard suggested that the party should proceed under the cover of a Red Cross flag, which they did as they left the hospital and walked into the battle zone. Kathleen Pierce and Louisa Nolan raced ahead of the party and out into the line of fire.

Despite the cease-fire, the fighting started up again as the two women began to help the wounded. When the doctors arrived at the scene they sought assurance from Reynolds at Clanwilliam House that the firing would cease. He acknowledged their request. The hospital staff tended to the wounded and removed them to the hospital. Two members of the clergy, Fr McNevin and Fr McCann, also lent assistance. The lack of stretchers meant that many of the wounded had to be carried off the road by the doctors and nurses. The ceasefire was to be short-lived.[22]

The British soldiers used the ceasefire to their advantage and started manoeuvring to take up better positions. This attempt was noted by the garrison at Clanwilliam House. Another blast on a whistle sounded and the Sherwood Foresters charged down Northumberland Road once again. As they ran they shouted 'good old Notts' before the Volunteers opened fire on them. At Clanwilliam House, Reynolds shouted to his men to be careful of the nurses and doctors who continued to tend to the wounded. As the last Foresters reached the bridge, Reynolds and the other Volunteers emptied the contents of their revolvers into the charging British soldiers. None of the soldiers reached his objective.

Next, Clanwilliam House came under machine-gun fire and, as the Volunteers took cover, the room was riddled with bullets. Doors were torn off their hinges, lumps of plaster and woodwork flew about the room and a piano in the corner played a sorry tune as the bullets hit it.[23] The Volunteers surmised that the British had mounted a machine gun in the bell tower of the church in Haddington Road, an elevated position that now gave them the advantage. For the remainder of the battle this merciless fire was kept up against Reynolds and his men.

Lieutenant Colonel Oates received orders from Brigadier Colonel Maconchy that a company from the 2/8th was to attempt another outflanking manoeuvre. The 2/8th had so far not been involved in the battle and was still in reserve at St Mary's Road. Oates was ordered to detach A Company under Captain Quibell and, by following the same route that Captain Wright had taken earlier, move around Beggars Bush barracks and attempt to move on the bridge via the right flank. Regimental histories for the Sherwood Foresters are somewhat contradictory, as they state that Captain Quibell's company was to move out via Serpentine Avenue, to take the electric power station from the rear and, if possible, to press on to occupy Lansdowne Road station.[24] This version of events suggests that the British soldiers would have travelled away from the bridge and not towards their enemy's known positions.

As the soldiers moved out they were suddenly recalled, as an important order came through from Irish high command. Brigadier General Lowe ordered that there were to be no diversionary tactics and that the battalion was to press the attack frontally towards the Grand Canal.[25] The tone of the order was one of impatience – Brigadier Lowe was under the impression that the Sherwood Forester regiment was making a big deal out of removing a handful of rebels from a schoolhouse. Having received this order, Brigadier Colonel Maconchy decided to move forward and check out the situation himself. He rode out on horseback from his headquarters at Pembroke town hall towards Northumberland Road. Waving crowds greeted him as he rode through the area; it was clear where the sympathies of the locals lay. Arriving at Northumberland Road he was briefed by Lieutenant Colonel Fane. No attempt to belittle the gravity of the situation was made by the lieutenant colonel, who claimed that the 2/7th could not take the bridge without support. He suggested that the 2/8th would also have to be brought into the fray.

Maconchy returned to his headquarters and relayed the present situation on Northumberland Road to General Lowe. Maconchy stated that the bridge could be taken but that it would take the remainder of the 2/7th as well as the 2/8th to complete the task. He also reiterated that it would involve heavy casualties. He asked Lowe if the situation demanded taking the bridge at all costs.

Lowe replied that it did – at all costs.[26]

7

WEDNESDAY, 26 APRIL 1916 EVENING

After his conversation with General Lowe, Brigadier General Maconchy summoned Lieutenant Colonel Oates of the 2/8th battalion to his headquarters at Pembroke town hall. He gave Oates a brief summary of the situation and how the 2/7th Sherwood Foresters had suffered appalling casualties. He then ordered Oates to 'go on with the job'. The exact orders that were given are reproduced in the regiment's history: 'Your battalion will storm the Mount Street Schools at all costs, at all costs mind, penetrate further if you can.'[27]

Captain Pragnell, who had been sent to reinforce Major Hanson along the canal bank, met the same fate as his predecessor. As he and his men moved from the shelter of Percy Lane out into Percy Place they were fired upon by the Volunteers at Clanwilliam House and also by the contingent in Roberts' yard. George Reynolds had already impressed upon his men the importance of Percy Lane and now every Volunteer fired at the British soldiers emerging from the laneway. This was the escape route for the Volunteers at 25 Northumberland Road and also for those in the parochial hall. As Captain Pragnell reached the bridge he took cover but was severely wounded and soon lost consciousness.

The Sherwood Foresters continued to charge the bridge at twenty-minute intervals, each attempt announced by the blast of a British officer's whistle. As they raced headlong into the sights of the Volunteers they suffered appalling casualties. Doctors and nurses from Sir Patrick Dun's hospital moved out to assist the wounded. Within twenty minutes the scenario would be repeated. Occasionally a number of British soldiers managed to cross the bridge but, lacking officers, they could only seek cover in the low-lying canal bank walls. Many of these men were wounded and the Volunteers at Roberts' yard often ceased firing to let the Foresters take more adequate cover under Mount Street Bridge.

At 5 p.m. Captain Jeffares of the Elm Park Bombing School of Instruction arrived. Armed with an ample supply of explosives, machine guns and experienced men, he set about planning his attack. Within the next thirty minutes three assaults were launched against 25 Northumberland Road. A grenade was thrown through a window and landed near a bed that contained over five hundred rounds of ammunition. Malone and Grace took cover as it exploded, destroying the room. They continued to fire on their attackers, moving from the front to the side of the house to discourage the attacking 2/7th from outflanking them. In one of these assaults Corporal H. Hutchinson and Private J.E. Booth, both of the 2/7th, managed to affix guncotton to the front door of Lieutenant Malone's position. The door was blown in and B Company of the Sherwood Foresters entered the house. Once inside, the soldiers could not proceed further as the stairs had been barricaded. Malone and Grace opened fire on the attackers, inflicting heavy casualties once again. The only option left was to withdraw from the hallway. Malone and Grace continued firing as the soldiers withdrew.

Inside 25 Northumberland Road, both Volunteers knew that it was only a matter of time before the British would successfully assault their position. Seamus Grace estimated that the final assault occurred at about 8.30 p.m. but the British army stated that it was just after 6 p.m. The final moments in 25 Northumberland Road were recorded by Grace. Malone ordered Grace down to the ground floor. As Grace waited in the hallway for Malone to join him, he saw a door handle turning. He fired into the door and then heard the sound of crashing glass as the back entrance was breached. British soldiers began pouring into the house. Grace opened fire in the direction of the assaulting troops and then proceeded to take cover in the basement of the house. Grace heard Malone shouting 'All right Seamus, I'm coming'. Shots rang out and Grace could hear a lot of activity on the stairway. British voices shouted 'Get him, get him'. A number of shots rang out. It is possible that these were the ones that killed Malone as he descended the stairway, his pipe in his mouth. Grace, having taken cover in the basement, continued to fire on the attacking British soldiers. But then his gun jammed and, as he attempted to cool the barrel under a water tap, two hand grenades were thrown into the basement. He took cover behind the cooker and as the grenades exploded the cellar was plunged into darkness. The British soldiers who entered the basement came within inches of their quarry but failed to find him. He stayed behind the relative safety of the cooker as the battle continued outside.

Post number one had fallen.[28]

The Volunteers at the parochial hall held out until about 6 p.m. Having fired their last few rounds the men decided to withdraw from their position. British forces had finally located their post and the assaults on the hall were becoming more frequent and were also accompanied by grenade attacks. However, as the Volunteers departed the building and made their way out into Percy Lane at the rear of the hall they were captured by British soldiers.

On being searched, Joe Clarke was found in possession

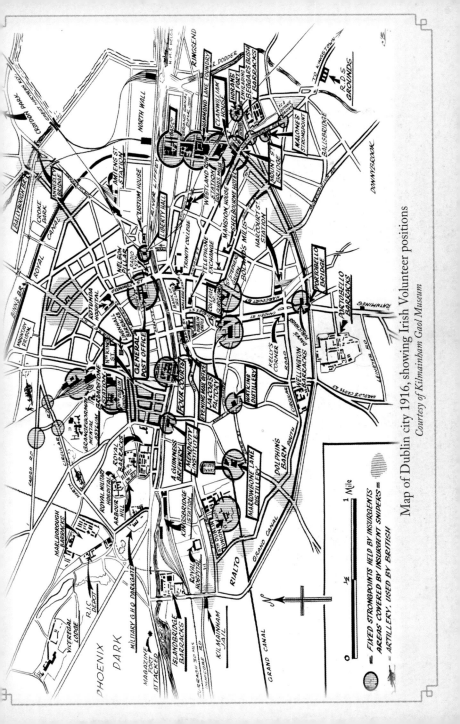

Map of Dublin city 1916, showing Irish Volunteer positions

Courtesy of Kilmainham Gaol Museum

LT. H.A Hewitt
Courtesy of the WFR Museum
(Sherwood Foresters Collection)

Arthur Annan Dickson
Courtesy of the WFR Museum
(Sherwood Foresters Collection)

Captain F.C Dietrichsen, one of
the first to be killed
Courtesy of the WFR Museum
(Sherwood Foresters Collection)

Captain Quibell
Courtesy of the WFR Museum
(Sherwood Foresters Collection)

The wife and children of Irish Volunteer Patrick Doyle
who was killed in action in Clanwilliam house
Courtesy of Kilmainham Gaol Museum

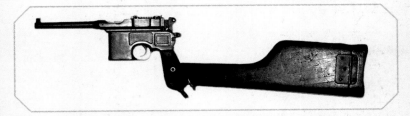

Mauser automatic pistol similar to that used by Michael Malone
Courtesy of Kilmainham Gaol Museum

Clanwilliam House after the battle
It was from the centre window that George Reynolds commanded the approach to the bridge during the battle

Memorial to the 3rd Batt., Irish
Volunteers in Ballsbridge
Courtesy of irishwarmemorials.com

Memorial to the men who fought
and died on Mount Street Bridge
Courtesy of irishwarmemorials.com

The stonebreakers yard in Kilmainham
gaol where the executions of the
leaders of the 1916 Rising took place
Courtesy of Kilmainham Gaol Museum

Plaque on the wall of 25 Northumberland Road in
memory of Michael Malone

Courtesy of irishwarmemorials.com

Malone's gravestone at Glasnevin cemetery in Dublin

Author's Collection

Claims for loss of property in the Mount Street
area of the city
Courtesy of Kilmainham Gaol Museum

25 Northumberland Road (Malone's position)
Courtesy of the Sean O'Mahony Collection

Michael Malone

Courtesy of UCD Archives (de Valera Papers, P150/504)

Scene taken from the television
programme 'Insurrection 1966'
© *RTÉ Stills Library*

Clanwilliam House where Irish volunteers and Sherwood Foresters
lost their lives in the battle

Courtesy of Kilmainham Gaol Museum

Bullet holes in the windows of Carrisbrook House

Courtesy of the Sean O'Mahony Collection

of a revolver. With his hands above his head he was placed in front of a backyard wooden door. A British officer drew his service revolver, aimed at Joe's head and squeezed the trigger. The bullet missed its victim and pierced the door. A British army doctor rushed out through the doorway and shouted abuse at the officer who fired the shot. He was using the back garden of the house as a makeshift field hospital. He instructed the officer to place the Volunteers under arrest and they were then escorted away to Lad Lane barracks.

Post number two had fallen.[29]

At St Mary's Road the 2/8th Sherwood Foresters waited in reserve. At 5.50 p.m. Colonel Oates assembled his officers and senior NCOs for their briefing. The plan of attack is detailed in the regimental histories of both battalions:

> Round the bend of the road, on the right, are the school and several houses strongly held. These must be taken tonight at all costs. B Company will lead; A Company will be in close support to press the attack home, C Company in Reserve. Start in three minutes – once under fire move quickly.[30]

Colonel Oates and Brigadier Maconchy moved along Northumberland Road. By 6 p.m. both officers had reached the junction of Northumberland Road and Haddington Road. They stood at the intersection and surveyed the roadway through the smoke of battle. By this time,

25 Northumberland Road had been silenced, as had the parochial hall. Lieutenant Harold Charles Daffen led B Company 2/8th along the west side of the roadway and immediately came under sustained fire from Clanwilliam House. Their advance was stopped opposite the school. A Company, under the command of Quibell, came up in support. Realising that B Company was taking heavy fire on the left side of the road, Quibell moved his men over to the right side and Lieutenant Foster followed.

As each company halted and took up position, the troops opened fire on Clanwilliam House. Foster and his men then stormed the schoolhouse. They entered through a window, expecting a fight at close quarters. However, they found only the dead bodies of the caretaker and his wife – the Volunteers had long since vacated the position. The company then moved out of the schoolhouse and took up a good strategic position facing Clanwilliam Terrace – the only obstacle between Clanwilliam House and the Sherwood Foresters was a small wall and the canal.

Lieutenant Foster ordered his men to open fire on Clanwilliam House. To his annoyance the first volley of shots missed the house completely. It was Corporal Warren who took the brunt of the abuse from the Lieutenant: 'How is it that normally this platoon has plenty of excellent marksmen and first class shots and yet now you can't hit a whole terrace at fifty yards' range?'[31] The soldiers continued to load their weapons, pull back the bolts and fire, and as they did, their marksmanship improved.

Then, with a blast on his whistle, Lieutenant Daffen led his men on a charge across the bridge. Once again, they were met by a hail of bullets. Daffen, only twenty-three years old, was killed almost immediately. His supporting officer, Lieutenant Montague Bernard Brown, was severely wounded, and died on 30 April. The 2/8th Sherwood Foresters were driven back across the bridge having once again failed to seize their objective.

At 7 p.m. and after a brief lull, the machine gunner in the bell tower of the church at Haddington Road opened fire on Clanwilliam House.[32] The bullets tore into the rooms and the Volunteers found it difficult to return fire on their attackers in the streets below. George Reynolds noticed that British soldiers were emerging from Percy Lane out into Percy Place. They took up position along the canal wall and started firing on Clanwilliam House. Reynolds ordered his men to continue firing to prevent the escape route for Malone and Grace at 25 Northumberland Road from being sealed. He did not realise that this position had already fallen and that his close friend Malone lay dead.

Reynolds suggested a two-man sortie from Clanwilliam House to Warrington Place, where they could take up a position opposite Percy Lane and open fire at the advancing Sherwood Foresters. His hope was to drive the British from their position and reopen the escape route for their comrades. But as Reynolds contemplated this idea the machine gunner in the bell tower opened fire once again; he realised the plan was futile and abandoned it. He and his men reloaded and awaited another assault on their position – an assault they knew was sure to come.

The 2/8th Sherwood Foresters continued the attack on Mount Street Bridge and, like their predecessors, the 2/7th, they suffered many casualties. As each assault took place the British succeeded in getting closer to their objective. After one such attack the soldiers managed to reach the railings of Clanwilliam House and hurl grenades against the wall of the building before they were driven back. Another group managed to cross the bridge and find shelter behind a large advertising hoarding. Though they were not in a great firing position they managed to draw the fire of the Volunteers who fired blindly into the hoarding.

Inside Clanwilliam House Reynolds ordered his men to pass him their weapons for cleaning as Jimmy Doyle's Martini Henry had jammed. The men watched from their posts as the attacks continued and the ranks of the khaki-clad soldiers grew in strength. Clanwilliam House had been riddled with bullets and the furniture and walls began to resemble sieves. With concentrated rifle fire coming from the British troops on either side of the bridge and the chatter of machine-gun fire from the bell tower, the garrison at Clanwilliam House found it increasingly difficult to return fire in any effective manner. Reynolds despatched Jimmy Doyle and Willie Ronan to the floor above to draw some of the fire away from the drawing-room. As they crawled from the room to the landing they discovered that the stairs had been shot away and that the walls of the landing, as well as some of the steps, had been obliterated by the intense firing. A water pipe had been shot through and water gushed into the house. Plaster-work lay strewn along the floor and bullets ricocheted off the walls. Both men pressed themselves against the wall and inched their way upstairs.

On reaching the room above, Willie Ronan took up his position in a room overlooking Mount Street Bridge. Jimmy Doyle occupied a position at the side of the house that looked out on to Warrington Place and the canal bank. Beyond this stretch of water he could see Percy Place. Around them, the firing became so intense that the furniture began to smoulder as the bullets tore through the fabrics.

Over the din of battle Patrick Doyle shouted, 'Boys, isn't this a great day for Ireland?'

Tom Walsh replied, 'Isn't it that!' and continued firing.

Doyle then said: 'Did I ever think I'd see a day like this? Shouldn't we all be grateful to the good God that he has allowed us to take part in a fight like this?'

The conversation was suddenly cut short as Doyle was shot through the head and killed.[33] As they removed him from his position and laid him down, the Walsh brothers and Dick Murphy said a short prayer.[34] In an effort to deceive the British, Tom Walsh placed a dressmaker's dummy in the window where his friend had been firing from moments before. Within seconds it was riddled with bullets as the room was raked by rifle and machine-gun fire. Furniture was set alight and the men had to use water siphons to extinguish the flames. Dick Murphy was shot dead as another fusillade of bullets swept the room. The Volunteers could hear the ever-increasing frequency of whistles being blown along the canal bank. Reynolds heard a voice shouting 'surrender' from outside the front of the house. He drew his revolver, fired in the direction that the voice had come from and moved upstairs to check on Ronan and Doyle.

Members of the 2/8th Sherwood Foresters were still pinned down on either side of the canal and also on the bridge. Lieutenant Hewitt ordered his men to open fire on the windows of Clanwilliam House. B Company had been totally wiped out – all its officers, NCOs and men were either killed or wounded. The reserve C Company, led by Captain F. Cursham, had been brought forward and now entered the fight. As they began to advance, their adjutant, Captain A.B. Leslie Melville, was severely wounded.

The British were forced back, suffering more fatalities as they retreated. Captain Cursham halted at the schoolhouse and linked up with Captain Quibell, Captain Cooper and Lieutenant Foster as well as some troops from the 2/7th. They proceeded slowly towards the bridge via the schoolhouse and towards the canal bank, emerging opposite Simon Donnelly's position at Roberts' yard. The Sherwood Foresters' view of Clanwilliam House was blocked by the advertising hoarding but, equally, the Volunteers inside the house could not fire directly into the British ranks as their view was also blocked. The British plan was once again to assault the enemy position by running the gauntlet of Mount Street Bridge.

Within the walls of Clanwilliam House the situation was becoming desperate. The Walsh brothers found it impossible to continue the rate of fire against their attackers and decided to withdraw out onto the landing. Jimmy Doyle had positioned himself on a table that gave him a good shot out towards Percy Lane. Suddenly an explosion knocked him unconscious and, when he came to, he found George Reynolds standing over him. The stock of Doyle's Martini Henri rifle had split due to his rapid firing and the weapon had overheated. As Doyle wiped the blood from his face, Reynolds told him to get another rifle and continue the fight.

Both men could hear the sounds of explosions below and Reynolds went out to the landing to investigate. Willie Ronan shouted to his comrades that the house was on fire. Doyle scrambled to the room from where Ronan's voice had come and both men attempted to extinguish the blaze. Reynolds called for assistance and as Doyle made his way out to the landing he saw Reynolds pointing to the door where the Wilson family had placed their valuables. Smoke was bellowing from under the doorway. They forced the door open and retrieved the family suitcases. As they returned to fight, Doyle told Reynolds that he was running low of ammunition; Reynolds assured him that reinforcements and ammunition were on the way. As Doyle took up his position he noted that the British troops had advanced to Warrington Place and were now firing from the low canal bank wall. They surveyed the mass of khaki-clad troops. A large group had amassed just over the bridge and it looked as if a major attack was imminent.

8

WEDNESDAY, 26 APRIL 1916 THE FINAL HOUR

As the Sherwood Foresters emerged from the cover of the schoolhouse, they came under fire from the Volunteers in Roberts' yard. Simon Donnelly's men had kept up a fierce rate of fire against the attackers. Their position frustrated attempts by the British to reach the canal bank via Pembroke Cottages. Donnelly's men were exhausted and had not had any water throughout the day-long battle. Lying exposed on the roof of the buildings that dominated the approach from the schoolhouse to the canal bank, they fired into the ranks of the British troops as they raced to the canal wall and took up a position that enabled them to assault the bridge when the order was given.

Though the Sherwood Foresters suffered heavy casualties, they still managed to move out from the schoolhouse to the canal wall. They took cover behind the hoarding and waited. Colonel Oates moved up Northumberland Road with six men and set up a field of covering fire from some stone steps. Captain Quibell shouted to Lieutenant Hewitt that they were preparing to move forward. Covering fire was directed at their objective and Captain Quibell led the charge across the bridge, closely followed by Lieutenants Hewitt and Foster and the men of C Company. Sergeant Major Dixie was shot dead and Captain Cursham of C Company and Lieutenant Curtis were wounded as they filed onto the bridge.

As they charged across the bridge the Sherwood Foresters were once again met by a hail of bullets fired by the defenders of Clanwilliam House. Lieutenant Foster recalled the moment: 'It was a bad moment, all we could do was sham dead and lie still.'[35] He reached out and took hold of a rifle that lay discarded on the bridge. As the firing from the house subsided, Captain Quibell leapt to his feet and shouted: 'Up and at them, lads.' On reaching the house they discovered that the building was heavily fortified. They flung grenades at the windows and doors in a desperate attempt to gain entry. Captain Cursham threw one at a window but it bounced back towards him, exploding and causing him fatal injuries. Captain Quibell had been wounded and passed the mantle of command to Lieutenant Foster, who pressed home the attack. By breaking a window Lieutenant Foster succeeded in forcing his way in.

George Reynolds, hearing the explosions below and the sound of hob-nailed boots on the pathway outside, decided to withdraw from the house. He shouted to his Volunteers: 'Come on lads, we can't do any more.' The explosions had caused the plasterwork to come crashing down and the house filled with smoke. British voices shouting 'Surrender, surrender!' were getting ever closer. Willie Ronan and Jimmy Doyle could hear Tom Walsh shouting to them to 'come on and get out'.

Reynolds and Tom Walsh were desperately firing into the ranks of the charging British soldiers as they came across the bridge. The British were so close now that Reynolds drew his revolver and emptied its contents into the advancing figures. As he stood up he was shot and fatally wounded. Tom Walsh came to Reynold's aid and saw that he had been shot in the thigh. Reynold's was still conscious as Doyle and Ronan entered the room. Both men saw that he had been badly wounded. They believed the roof of the house was on fire and urged everyone to make a break from the building. Meanwhile, Tom Walsh tried in vain to stem Reynold's bleeding.

As Ronan and Jimmy Doyle looked around the room they saw Patrick Doyle lying dead on his side and the body of Dick Murphy, rifle in hands, propped by the window, still facing the enemy. They moved Reynolds onto the landing and Tom Walsh whispered an act of contrition in his ear. Reynolds asked for a drink of water, which they gave him from a bowl that was in the room, even though it was dirty from bits of fallen plaster and dust. They helped Reynolds to drink, and as he finished his last words were 'God' and 'Mick, Mick'. His head fell to one side and he died.

The other Volunteers could hear the wild cheering of their attackers outside as the explosions continued to rock the house. With their section commander dead, the remaining four Volunteers, Willie Ronan, James Doyle, and Thomas and James Walsh retreated to the basement through the kitchen. The back door had been barricaded and the men could not remove the obstacles. They found a small square window about one foot wide and each man squeezed through and made his way out into the back garden. They scaled the garden wall and as they fell into the lane on the other side they dispersed in separate directions.[36]

Once Lieutenant Foster and Captain Quibell gained entry to the house, Foster went quickly upstairs. As he reached the landing he saw a figure standing there at the turn in the stairway. Foster shot at the figure and claimed that the figure returned fire. He fired again and then bayoneted the man. That figure may have been George Reynolds. With the smoke, heat and confusion of battle, Lieutenant Foster may have believed he was under fire from a man that had already been left for dead. The fire within the house had probably ignited ammunition and, with the sound of gunfire, explosions and men shouting, the scene was one of utter chaos.

Proceeding through the house, Foster opened the drawing-room door and saw the bodies of two men he believed were still alive and firing at his men below. He hurled a hand grenade into the room and closed the door; after the explosion he opened the door and saw the two bodies lying on the floor. The grenade had ruptured a gas pipe and a great mass of flame filled the room. As he composed himself, his men entered the building and began throwing grenades into each room in an attempt to clear the house of its occupants. Foster made his way outside into the street and gazed back at Clanwilliam House, which was now burning fiercely. Major Rayner turned to him and said: 'Perhaps we ought to send for the fire brigade.'

In reply somebody asked: 'How does one send for the fire brigade?'

Foster erupted into laughter as the silhouette of the burning house lit up the Dublin skyline.

Post number three had fallen.

9
WEDNESDAY, 26 APRIL 1916 NIGHTFALL

As nightfall slowly descended, the sound of gunfire and explosions continued as British troops stormed suspected strongholds. They found nothing except a terrified population, many of them relieved that the British soldiers had taken control of the area and hoping that normality would return to this quiet and leafy part of Dublin.

The night sky was illuminated by the fires in Clanwilliam House and the blaze soon spread to the house next door. The occupants, Mr and Mrs Mathis, emerged from their basement where they had taken shelter during the fighting; they sat in the garden and watched their house burn to the ground. Local residents brought ham and cups of tea for the troops as they rested after the battle. Brigadier Maconchy rode on horseback from his headquarters at Pembroke town hall to Mount Street Bridge. The route was lined by soldiers with fixed bayonets, while locals emerged from their houses cheering the brigadier as he rode by.

Orders had been received from Irish high command to consolidate on the line of the canal. The Sherwood Foresters took up positions to secure the bridge and its surroundings. The area from Mount Street Bridge to Grand Canal Street was held by B Company, commanded by Bandmaster Cooper. This section was under fire, possibly from the contingent of Volunteers at Boland's bakery. The British troops used pieces of turf to barricade their position and make it tenable. The buildings at Percy Place were taken over by the men of A and C Companies. The nearest the Sherwood Foresters got to their original objective of Trinity College was Merrion Square, where they placed pickets. The remainder of the battalion occupied the schoolhouse, where many took the opportunity to get some sleep. Battalion headquarters was moved from the town hall to 23 Northumberland Road.

It was 2 a.m. on Thursday before the Sherwood Foresters were relieved by the Staffordshire regiment. The remainder of the Sherwood Foresters made their way back to the Royal Dublin Horse Society to eat and rest. Here they were joined by the second-in-command Captain Martyn and D Company, who had arrived via the SS *The Ulster*. The battle for Northumberland Road and Mount

Street Bridge had finally come to an end. Though the Rising continued until the end of the week, the British army did not suffer as many losses as it had in its attempt to take the schoolhouse and the bridge. The total number of British casualties was not immediately known as many of the dead and wounded had been taken to the nearby Sir Patrick Dun's hospital. Later it emerged that four officers were killed, and fourteen wounded; 216 men of other ranks were killed or wounded – all in a single day of fighting at Mount Street Bridge.

The soldiers made their way to the Royal Hospital at Kilmainham via South Circular Road and, as they reached Rialto Bridge, the 2/8th battalion of the Sherwood Foresters came under fire from Commandant Éamonn Ceannt's men who were positioned in Marrowbone Lane distillery and the South Dublin Union. The battalion halted and sought assistance from Portobello barracks in Rathmines.

Major Sir Francis Vane soon arrived with fifty men and discovered that the column was escorting an important consignment of ammunition. Vane described the Sherwood Foresters as being very inexperienced and Colonel Oates as being very 'distracted'.[37] Instead of moving around or avoiding the Irish Volunteer positions, Vane moved forward with two companies of the Foresters and his own fifty men in an attempt to dislodge the Volunteers. They entered the grounds of the South Dublin Union and gained access to the main nurses' home.

Captain Martyn and D company assisted in the assault of the South Dublin Union, where a close-quarter struggle with rifle, grenade and revolver fire lasted until evening. In one attack on a rebel-held building, a grenade was thrown at the Volunteer positions but it rolled back towards the British soldiers. Martyn rushed forward, seized the explosive device and hurled it towards the enemy.

The 2/8th Sherwood Foresters suffered heavy losses once again. Within the South Dublin Union it is estimated that the Volunteer force numbered just twenty-seven, and it was here that Cathal Brugha of the Irish Volunteers distinguished himself in defence of the building. The British forces eventually withdrew and Brigadier Maconchy proceeded to the Royal Hospital at Kilmainham. The Volunteers continued to snipe as the battalion made the tedious journey, but the British did not encounter any more heavy opposition. Many of the soldiers were billeted in the courtyard of the hospital while others rested in the great hall and chapel.

Meanwhile, at Clanwilliam House, Willie Ronan and the two Walsh brothers scaled the garden wall at the rear of the house and made their way through the back gardens until they came to Love Lane. In need of clothing to cover their uniforms, they knocked on the door of a house. A young girl appeared, but when they asked for some clothes her mother shouted that they would all be shot if they gave the Volunteers assistance.[38] They continued on their way through the gardens until they discovered an empty basement flat, where they found some discarded clothing. Disguised in female coats, a tramway uniform and an overcoat, they made their way to Mount Street. They could still hear the distant rumble of explosions and shots being fired. The street was crowded with curious onlookers. On seeing a friend, Tom Walsh told him they were going to take shelter in a nearby stable and to tell his mother that they needed food and clothing. Later, Mrs Walsh arrived with new clothing and food and the three Volunteers, well-fed and warm, made their way into the grounds of a nearby convent. Early the following morning they left the safety of the convent grounds and headed for a 'safe house' that Mrs Walsh had arranged for them.

James Doyle had also successfully escaped from Clanwilliam House as the British stormed the building. He was shot at but managed to evade his pursuers. A hostile crowd attacked him near Merrion Square but he fought them off and reached Stephen's Place, where he collapsed from exhaustion. A sympathetic crowd carried him to a house, where his wounds were dressed and he rested in relative safety.

James Grace, who had hidden behind the cooker in the basement of 25 Northumberland Road, left the basement and hid in a coal shed as the British troops pressed home their attack on the other posts. Later that night he attempted to swim across the canal with his boots tied around his neck. He almost made it across but was challenged by guards who had been posted along the canal bank. He retreated to the coal shed where he stayed for almost three days. He was eventually discovered by a British army patrol and placed under arrest.[39]

The other Volunteers at the parochial hall had all been placed under arrest after they vacated the post, and in the coming days they faced deportation to prisons in Britain. Joe Clarke, like many others, was escorted to Wakefield prison and then Frongoch prison camp in Wales.[40]

Lieutenant Michael Malone was buried in the garden of 25 Northumberland Road, with his face covered by a handkerchief. Later it was exhumed and reburied at Glasnevin cemetery.

The fire at Clanwilliam House was so intense that no remains were recovered from the ashes, except for a single human bone. The bodies of George Reynolds, Patrick Doyle and Richard Murphy were consumed within the flames. Though the Irish Volunteers wanted their ranks to consist of young, unmarried men, this was not the case with Patrick Doyle. His death left behind a widow and five young children.

MAY 1916 – EXECUTIONS AT KILMAINHAM GAOL

Official War Office records dating from 2 May 1916 detail the procedures that were carried out in relation to the prisoners executed for their involvement in the rebellion. These orders were hastily improvised and were written by Brigadier J. Young, headquarters Irish command at Parkgate. They were then sent to Major General A.E. Sandbach, the general officer commanding the troops in Dublin. These were issued quickly as it was expected that a large number of prisoners would be executed in the days following the court-martials. Ninety-seven men were condemned to death but only sixteen were ultimately executed – fourteen in Kilmainham gaol, one in Cork and one in London. As news of the executions spread, popular opinion swung massively in favour of the Irish Volunteers, which put pressure on the authorities to stop the executions.

The minutes circulated by military command stated:

In the event of the Sinn Féin prisoners being condemned to death today, they will be segregated (so far as circumstances permit) and asked whether they want to see relatives or friends or chaplains; and these persons will be sent for as required by the prisoners. A number of motor cars will be stationed at Richmond barracks for this purpose, and more may be asked for from HQ Irish Command, as necessary.

The whole of the visitors and friends are to be taken back to their homes before 3.30 a.m. the next day, at which time the first firing party will parade. The first man to be shot will be brought out at 3.45 a.m. facing the firing party officer and twelve men at ten paces distant. [It was light then as daylight saving did not come into operation in Ireland until 21 May 1916 and GMT was not introduced until 1917.]

The rifles of the firing party will be loaded by other men behind their backs, one rifle with blank cartridge, and eleven with ball and the firing party will be told that this is the arrangement, and no man is to know which rifle is loaded with a blank. There will be four firing parties who will fire in turn.[41]

Soldiers from the Sherwood Forester regiment made up the firing squads. Captain H.M. Whitehead, 7th battalion Sherwood Foresters, was the acting assistant provost marshal. His signature appears on many documents relating to the executions at Kilmainham gaol.[42]

One of those involved in the executions was Captain Arthur Annan Dickson, who joined the officer training corps in 1915, having previously been employed by Lloyds bank at Holsworthy (in Devon). Early in 1916 he was commissioned into the 2/7th Nottingham and Derbyshire battalion (Sherwood Foresters), stationed at Watford. Captain Dickson recorded his own personal involvement in the Rising of 1916, from his first action at the battle of Mount Street Bridge to his direct involvement in the executions that took place in the stone-breakers yard of Kilmainham gaol.

Captain Dickson received his orders regarding the assembly of a firing squad from Major Harold Heathcote, officer in charge of prisoners. Dickson's lack of knowledge of the city of Dublin is reflected in a statement in which he confuses Kilmainham gaol with Mountjoy prison. His account reads:

The Court Martial at Richmond Barracks sentenced many of the rebels to imprisonment and a number of the leaders to death. One evening five subalterns were ordered to command firing parties to shoot five of them in Mountjoy Jail [Kilmainham] the following dawn. A kindly but strict old Major [Heathcote] of one of the other battalions gave detailed instructions to each of us.

I was to march my firing squad of a sergeant and twelve men to a point cut off from the execution point by a projecting wall; halt them to ground arms there; march them forward twelve paces to halt with their backs to their rifles each of which I was to load and replace on the ground. Thus no man knew whether his rifle had been loaded with blank or with ball; each was therefore left not knowing whether he personally had shot the man or not. The men were then to be marched back to pick up their rifles and hold them at attention under my eye, until word came that the prisoner was to be led out; they must then be marched around and halted facing the execution wall.

A priest will accompany the prisoner, the Major told me and as the priest leaves him, you give the orders – Ready, Present, Fire. Then he emphasised, the men must not remain in sight of the prisoner; immediately you turn them about and march them back around the baffle wall. There they ground arms, you march them forward to halt facing away while you empty the breach of each rifle and collect the cartridge cases, all to be handed in after. Then march them back to pick up their rifles, clean them on the spot and the job is done.[43]

Captain Dickson was based at Richmond barracks, Inchicore, and Dublin as the court martial proceedings were taking place. He carried out daily inspections of the prisoners' quarters which, in fact, were merely over-crowded barrack rooms. He escorted Countess Markievicz and Countess Plunkett from Kilmainham gaol to Mountjoy prison. This took place during curfew and, as both ladies refused to take a cab under escort, they walked to Mountjoy under a guard of a half a dozen soldiers. The women's slow pace frustrated their military escort but they made their journey unhindered.

From here Countess Markievicz was sent to Aylesbury

gaol in England. However, Captain Dickson returned to Kilmainham gaol at dawn on 8 May 1916. Once again he mistook Kilmainham gaol for Mountjoy prison as he prepared his firing squad:

We marched our squads to Mountjoy Prison [Kilmainham Gaol] long before dawn in a dismal drizzle, but the men with memories of our losses seemed to have no qualms as to doing the job. 'Pity to dirty all these rifles; why can't we do him in with a bit of bayonet practice?' We had to wait while it grew faintly light and I took the chance to instruct the squad exactly what orders they would get; I didn't want any muddle about getting them back around the wall.

After 'ready', I told them on the word 'present' you bring your rifles smartly up to the standing-aim position, aiming at a piece of white paper pinned on his chest and on the word 'fire', a steady pressure on the trigger, just like on the range. Then at once I shall give you 'slope arms', 'about turn', then, as we clear this wall right incline, 'halt', 'ground arms'.

Thanks to the preparation it was carried out smoothly. The thirteen rifles went off in a single volley. The rebel dropped to the ground like an empty sack; I barked out 'slope arms, about turn, and quick march'. They marched in perfect order round the wall, grounded arms, and I told them 'right you made a good job of that gentlemen'. Remember we had all lost some good pals in our first day's active service. I can't say I felt much except that it was just another job that had to be done, though I was glad that there was no doubt the rifles had done their work and there was no need for me to do what the old Major had told me, about the officer going back and finishing the job with his revolver.[44]

All the firing squads were drawn from soldiers of the Sherwood Forester regiment and their regimental history states that 'all men met their fate bravely'.[45] The fourteen executions that took place at Kilmainham gaol involved over two hundred soldiers.

It was only on the first day of the executions, 3 May, that priests were prohibited from entering the stone-breakers yard to administer extreme unction. The clergy protested and as a result the procedures were changed and they were subsequently admitted into the yard.

That the condemned met their fate bravely is a fitting tribute to the Irish Volunteers and Citizen Army leaders who were executed. Participation in a firing squad must have haunted all those involved for decades after the event as they remembered staring down the barrels of their rifles at the blindfolded target. Many of the Volunteers had asked not to be blindfolded, but this request was not granted as the blindfold was used not only to protect the condemned from the action, but also to protect the men of the firing squad from looking into the eyes of those they were about to execute.

Father Aloysius praised some of the officers involved and highlighted their kindness to the condemned and their families.[46] Many British officers regretted their involvement in the trials and subsequent executions. Strict British military law and the obedience to orders not only enforced the ultimate sentence on the Irish Volunteers but also ensured that these new drafts of the British army would carry out the order or face a similar fate.

Indeed, carrying out orders had resulted in the Sherwood Foresters being at Kilmainham gaol and was also responsible for the heavy casualties they suffered during the battle for Mount Street Bridge.

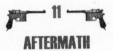

AFTERMATH

The Nottingham and Derbyshire battalion received a special message of thanks from General Sir John Maxwell, commander-in-chief of the British army in Ireland:

Towards evening the 178th Infantry Brigade began to arrive at Kingstown and in accordance with orders the brigade left Kingstown in two columns ... The right column consisting of the 7th and 8th Sherwood Foresters, by the main tram route through Ballsbridge, and directed on Merrion Square and Trinity College.

This column, with 7th battalion leading, was held up at the corner of Haddington Road and Northumberland Road ... the 7th battalion Sherwood Foresters met great opposition from the rebels holding the schools and other houses on the north side of the road close to the bridge at Lower Mount Street, and two officers, one of whom was Adjutant Captain Dietrichsen, were killed, and seven wounded, including Lieutenant Colonel Fane, who though wounded, remained in action.

At about 5.30 p.m. orders were received that the advance to Trinity College was to be pushed forward at all costs and therefore at about 8 p.m. after careful arrangements, the whole column, accompanied by bombing parties, attacked the schools and houses where the chief opposition lay, the battalions charging in successive waves, carried all before them, but, I regret to say, suffered severe casualties in doing so.

Four officers were killed, fourteen wounded and of the other ranks two hundred and sixteen were killed and wounded.

The steadiness shown by these two battalions is deserving of a special mention, as I understand the majority of men have less than three months' service.

In view of the opposition met with, it was not considered advisable to push on to Trinity College that night, so at 11 p.m. the 5th Staffordshire Regiment from the 176th infantry brigade, reinforced this column, and by occupying the position gained allowed the two battalions of Sherwood Foresters to be concentrated at Ballsbridge.[47]

For their gallantry at the battle of Mount Street Bridge a number of honours were awarded to the men of the regiment. The order of St Michael and St George was awarded to Major and Battalion Lieutenant Colonel Cecil Fane. Captain A.H. Quibell and Captain Rayner both received the Distinguished Service Order. Privates J. Hill, F. Snowdin, Sergeant R.M. Cooper and acting Sergeant Major T. Cumming all received the Distinguished Conduct Medal, while Second Lieutenants H.A. Hewitt and M.C. Martyn were awarded the Military Cross for their part in the action on Mount Street. Many others were mentioned in despatches, their deeds of gallantry being temporarily recorded but later forgotten as the casualties from the Great War mounted.

Miss Louisa Nolan, who assisted the wounded British troops on the bridge, was awarded the Military Medal.[48]

General Sir John Grenfell Maxwell issued the following despatch with regard to the heroism of those who attempted to give aid to the wounded at Mount Street:

> In connection with this fighting at Mount Street Bridge, where our heaviest casualties occurred, I should like to mention the gallant assistance given by a number of medical men, ladies, nurses and women servants, who at great risk brought in and tended the wounded, continuing their efforts even when deliberately fired at by the rebels.[49]

This accusation was refuted by Dr C.B. O'Brien, MD, who wrote the following letter to the newspapers:

> This despatch General Maxwell did not deign to support with any evidence, thinking that martial law would provide sufficient deterrent against contradiction or controversy of any kind. Having been present from start to finish at the hostilities at Mount Street Bridge Easter Week 1916 and having assisted in bringing in and attending the wounded in obedience to all the laws of honourable warfare, I feel it incumbent

on me to publish a dignified yet flat contradiction to this particular part of the despatch. There was no doctor, lady, nurse or ambulance attendant fired on or wounded by the rebels. On the contrary the valour, pluck and total disregard for personal safety whilst strictly observing to … the laws of open battle, was the impression carried home by those whose misfortune it was to be there.[50]

The Sherwood Foresters continued their service in Ireland. They took part in the battle to regain Dublin city, and in the days following the surrender, they escorted prisoners to England.[51] After the regiment took part in the executions at Kilmainham gaol during May 1916, its troops were posted to counties throughout the country to restore law and order and to enforce martial law, which had been declared by General Maxwell. After the Rising they began training for the war in France and, as soon as they returned to full strength, were sent to Flanders in early 1917. There they were to suffer even more casualties until the war ended in November 1918. In total, the Sherwood Foresters suffered 10,189 casualties during the Great War.

Captain Arthur Annan Dickson, the officer who commanded one of the firing squads, found himself in command of a trench mortar battery in France. Wounded a number of times, he was finally shot in the neck by a German sniper, a wound that resulted in him being sent back to England and being discharged from the army. After a lengthy recovery he returned to Lloyds bank and worked his way up to the position of manager. Having actively taken part in the battle for Dublin in 1916, the executions at Kilmainham gaol and the killing fields of France, Dickson became a Quaker and a pacifist in later life. His memories of his brief posting in Dublin during 1916 are contained within his service pocket book and a thirteen-page handwritten manuscript that is held at the Imperial War Museum, London. He died in 1979.[52]

Brigadier General Maconchy was appointed president of one of the field general courts martial in Dublin. He protested at this appointment, claiming he was an Irishman. He presided over the trials of Michael Mallin, William Pearse, Joseph Plunkett and Seán Heuston among others. In his memoir he states that he was relieved when an officer of the judge advocates department took over the post.[53]

Many civilians were killed or injured during the battle of Mount Street Bridge. Mrs Elizabeth Kane was killed and her daughter seriously wounded when their house, 20 Delahunty Buildings, came under fire. Mr Hayter, a local grocer, was killed as he attempted to cross the line of fire. Curious onlookers were caught in the crossfire and either killed or wounded. Many people left the shelter of their homes to assist the wounded British soldiers who lay exposed on Northumberland Road and Mount Street Bridge. Mr C. Hanchette Hyland was killed as he looked out the back door of 3 Percy Place. He was a dentist who had donned his white coat and gone out to give assistance to the wounded British soldiers on Mount Street Bridge. Having survived this courageous act, he was shot by a stray bullet as he stood in the doorway of his house.

The Volunteers at Roberts' yard withdrew back to Boland's bakery on orders from Simon Donnelly. There, Éamon de Valera and his men never received the full frontal assault on their position they had expected. Small skirmishes took place in the days that followed the fall of Clanwilliam House and the men holding Boland's bakery finally surrendered under orders from Patrick Pearse, commander-in-chief of the Irish Volunteers:

> In order to prevent the further slaughter of Dublin citizens, and in the hope of saving the lives of our followers now surrounded and hopelessly outnumbered, the members of the Provisional Government present at Headquarters have agreed to an unconditional surrender, and the commandants of the various districts in the city and country will order their commands to lay down arms. 29 April, 3.45 p.m., 1916.[54]

The Boland's bakery garrison was led away, passing over Mount Street Bridge and 25 Northumberland Road, to be held under guard at the Royal Dublin Showground.

In the years following the battle of Mount Street

Bridge many of the survivors remained active within the Irish Volunteers, and continued the struggle for Ireland's freedom during the War of Independence.

The Civil War that followed the War of Independence saw James Doyle refusing to take sides in that terrible tragedy. He was the last remaining survivor of the battle of Mount Street, and died in Baltinglass hospital, aged eighty-two. Joe Clarke continued his association with the republican movement until his death in April 1976. William Ronan died on 8 September 1965 having spent much of his life in mental institutions.[55] Simon Donnelly lived until he was seventy-five and recorded his participation in the battle for Mount Street in an unpublished manuscript, *They Shall Not Pass*.

Éamon de Valera was sentenced to be executed for his participation in the Rising but his death sentence was commuted to life imprisonment on 11 May 1916. He was, however, released almost a year later and continued the struggle against the British until the signing of the Treaty in 1921. In the Civil War he was on the republican side and found himself imprisoned in Kilmainham gaol in 1923. After the war he continued in politics and soon became taoiseach of Ireland and, later, the country's president.

Eoin MacNeill was arrested by the British as they attempted to suppress the Volunteers in the aftermath of the Rising and was sent to Dartmoor prison for a year.

On his release he joined the Sinn Féin government in 1918 and remained active in the political arena until he lost his parliamentary seat in 1927. He then returned to his academic profession until his death in 1945.

The Mauser automatic pistol used by Malone in the battle of Mount Street was taken as a war trophy by a British officer. Years later it was returned to Éamon de Valera by the British officer and the de Valera family handed it over to the gardaí for safe-keeping. In May 1999, the garda commissioner, Eugene Crowley, presented the weapon to the National Museum of Ireland at the behest of the de Valera family.

As Ireland emerged from the aftermath of those terrible years the men and women who had taken part in Ireland's fight for freedom attempted to reconstruct a country that had been almost destroyed by years of armed conflict.

12

APRIL 1916 – MILITARY SUCCESS AND MILITARY FAILURE

The strategy and tactics deployed by both sides during the 1916 Rising have been scrutinised by students of military history. A careful examination reveals three key points: the British high command reacted quickly to the events that were unfolding in Dublin city;[56] the Irish Volunteers showed great organisational ability and more military skill than they have been given credit for; and the battle for Mount Street Bridge can be considered a turning point in warfare. By examining the actions taken by both sides, one may conclude that the battle resulted in one of Ireland's greatest military actions and provided a glimpse of the future of modern warfare.

The difference between strategy and tactics can often be confused so we must differentiate between the two.

Strategy in war is often the formulation of policy. This can be divided into the aims of war, the establishment of alliances, both political and military, and also the gathering of resources to achieve one's objective. Tactics are the methods of fighting and deployment of those military resources in order to achieve one's objective.[57]

British high command in Ireland immediately reacted to the developing situation by implementing a plan to retake and secure the city of Dublin. Brigadier General W.H.M. Lowe took control in the absence of commander-in-chief Major General C.H. Friend, who was in England. Orders to carry out these tasks were relayed to the Curragh camp in Kildare, and the War Office in London was informed via a naval transmitter at Kingstown (Dún Laoghaire). This single action led to troops being moved from the Curragh camp to Dublin and the immediate mobilisation of the 178th brigade in England with orders to embark for Ireland.

The first tasks included the relief of Dublin Castle, a tightening of security around barracks and the erection of a cordon around the city. General Lowe had forced his way into the city by way of gunfire and artillery. The failure of the Irish Volunteers to secure Dublin Castle or Trinity College gave the British a direct route to the centre of the city. This enabled them to reinforce their positions and build up a force large enough to attack the Volunteers' defences. The British army was engaged in severe and brutal street fighting throughout the city. This type of warfare was new to the army, whose soldiers had never experienced such fighting during the nineteenth or early twentieth centuries. Trench warfare in France and Belgium was far removed from the street fighting in Dublin. At the time, British military strategy was dominated by offensive man-oeuvres that had been in practice since the 1870s. British campaigns of the latter part of the nineteenth century had been fought on the plains of Africa against poorly armed natives. It was only during the mutiny in India in 1857 that fighting occurred in built-up areas such as Delhi and Lucknow. During the Paris Commune of 1871, the French army had to regain the city by force. This defence and assault in a built-up area resulted in heavy casualties on both sides. The use of artillery to remove the defenders destroyed much of the city and inflicted significant losses on the civilian population. The government regained the city but at a high price.[58]

However, a situation unfolded in Britain during the early part of the twentieth century that mirrored what was to take place in Dublin in 1916. But the authorities failed to recognise and act upon this event, and it would later cost them dearly.

In London, on 2 January 1911, British metropolitan police surrounded 100 Sydney Street in the East End of the city. Following a failed robbery attempt in which a number of policemen had been killed, a group of Russian and Latvian anarchists had taken refuge in the building. They included Fritz Svaars, Joseph Marx and Peter Piatkov. The British police, armed with single-shot rifles with .22 calibre practice rounds as well as revolvers and shotguns, attempted to dislodge the anarchists from the building. The men in the house were armed with a variety of modern, high-velocity semi-automatic pistols that could be quickly reloaded.

The police, totally unprepared for such a scenario, suffered many fatalities. It was only when they were reinforced by members of the Scots Guards, despatched from the Tower of London, that they managed to put an end to the siege as the house caught fire and two revolutionaries were killed. Their charred bodies were found in the house. Peter Piatkov was presumed to have escaped as his body was never found. He received the nickname 'Peter the Painter' and has been associated with his weapon of choice, the 9mm Mauser automatic, ever since.

This fighting in a built-up area was witnessed by Winston Churchill, who was home secretary at the time.[59] Nonetheless, both the military and the government had failed to see the threat of warfare in a built-up area, and by 1916 the army was once again plunged into a situation where it lacked proper training and equipment.

The Sherwood Foresters who arrived in Dublin were inexperienced young men, having received just six weeks' training. They were not prepared for war on the Western

Front, let alone the events that were to unfold in Dublin. Though the rebellion was subdued within a week, with much credit for this being given to Generals Lowe and Friend, the tragic events that unfolded on Mount Street Bridge can also be blamed on the British high command. The failure to properly reconnoitre the area contributed greatly to the loss of life suffered by the Sherwood Forester regiment.

British commanders failed to exploit the terrain on which they were fighting, as they could have encircled the Volunteers by moving their forces through the streets either side of the bridge. This manoeuvre would have isolated and surrounded the Volunteers' outposts.

The official war histories state that the battle of Mount Street was not an ambush, as the battalion had received intelligence that the schoolhouse was occupied by rebel forces.[60] This schoolhouse was their main objective. They had no further information on the strength or number of the insurgents in the area. An ambush may be defined as an attack from a concealed position on an enemy that passes its location. In order to survive this tactic, the British forces should have withdrawn from the area the way they had entered – via Northumberland Road. A regrouping and further detailed reconnaissance of the area would have proved invaluable to the British command. This manoeuvre might have resulted in the preservation of a force that could then have been better deployed.

The inexperienced 2/7th and 2/8th repeatedly persisted with frontal assaults down Northumberland Road and onto Mount Street Bridge. This tactic of frontal assault is a direct move in large numbers towards the enemy force in an attempt to overwhelm it. Tacticians have called this manoeuvre the last resort of a commander as the results are often predictable and tragic.

Attempts to outflank the rebel positions were thwarted by the Irish Volunteers. Attacks would have been more effective if launched at the flanks of the Volunteers' positions. To achieve this, a unit would have attacked the Volunteers' positions with a suppressive fire, preventing them from returning fire or from leaving their fixed positions. The flanking movement would have involved British forces crossing other bridges (Baggot Street and Grand Canal Street) along the canal and moving down to Mount Street Bridge from each direction before attacking the flanks of the Irish Volunteer positions.

Though the Volunteers had these positions covered, they did not have the manpower or the resources to hold the flanks indefinitely against a close-range assault. However, the British commander on the ground at Mount Street asked if it was necessary to take the bridge, the schoolhouse and Clanwilliam House. He was ordered to take the objectives at all costs and was forbidden to make further attempts to outflank the rebel positions. It was this order, blindly followed, that resulted in the British forces in Dublin suffering their heaviest casualties on Mount Street Bridge.

The British were ill-equipped to deal with the Volunteers' defensive positions as they lacked hand grenades and machine-guns. The officer loading in England assured the battalion commanders that men were needed urgently. Lewis machine-gun units remained in Britain as they often consisted of twenty-six to thirty men: the ships bringing the reinforcements to Ireland could only cope with the infantry and not with the equipment and supplies needed for a machine-gun section. Ultimately, it took the deployment of machine guns and explosives to turn the tide on Mount Street in favour of the British.

A commander in battle is expected to use his own initiative when it comes to making military and tactical decisions, but little initiative was shown by the British officers during the battle of Mount Street. Military theory of the time favoured frontal assaults. The theory that an attacking force with superior numbers could turn the tide of battle seems to have been accepted by the British army until the battle of the Somme, which started on 1 July 1916.

The Irish Volunteers showed remarkable military competence during the 1916 rebellion. The occupation of key buildings in Dublin city and the military plan of the Volunteers are accredited to James Connolly and Joseph Plunkett. Little evidence is available to suggest that others were involved in the tactical planning of the rebellion. The deployment of the Volunteers throughout the city saw them secure two main posts on the north side, the General Post Office and the Four Courts, and four positions on the south side, South Dublin Union, Stephen's Green, Jacob's biscuit factory and Boland's bakery. Unfortunately, the countermanding order issued by Eoin Mac-Neill greatly reduced the strength of the Volunteers. The 3rd battalion under the command of Éamon de Valera mobilised at Great Brunswick Street and consisted of 130 men. If mobilised correctly, the total force should have been 400 men.[61] The area that this battalion had to cover was large and occupied posts on Northumberland Road and Mount Street.

Lieutenant Michael Malone deployed his forces in the area of Northumberland Road and Mount Street Bridge with brilliant tactical *nous*. The commander had analysed and understood his orders and had planned in advance for the engagement. Fighting in a built-up area favours the defenders, who are often forced to hold off an enemy with superior numbers. Malone's positions were well chosen, barricaded and overlooked a number of approaches to all of the occupied posts. He allotted different defensive areas to each section, not just to one frontal station. He chose a flexible strategy that could be changed to adapt to any conditions likely to be encountered.

When fighting in the built-up area around Mount Street, Malone engaged a number of tactics that are still in use today. He considered all avenues of approach to the area and positioned his men so that these areas were covered with a line of withdrawal available if needed. The terrain covered by his men included the bridge over the canal and Northumberland Road. The defenders positioned their weapons to obtain maximum effect and mutual supporting fire. This can be seen by the actions of the Volunteers at Clanwilliam House who engaged the enemy over a long range and had a clear field of fire. In cover and concealment, their positions were well chosen and well defended as the Volunteers reinforced their stations with the materials at hand. The posts remained concealed until the enemy was engaged. With a limited number of men, Malone concentrated his resources at a decisive point; an offensive by the Volunteers would have needed greater manpower, which was unavailable. Malone's men were well armed and well trained in the use of their weapons. The Volunteers also expected their attackers to use incendiary devices and were prepared for this with siphons filled with water.

Unfair criticism is often levelled against Commandant Éamon de Valera for his failure to reinforce the garrisons at Northumberland Road. Some historians believe that a sortie from the bakery may have turned the tide of battle and resulted in defeat of the British forces. However, the Volunteers' defensive zone was sensible and well structured. The 3rd battalion was seriously under strength and to hold Boland's bakery and to reinforce those forward positions Éamon de Valera would have needed a larger number of men. The force at Clanwilliam House, the parochial hall and 25 Northumberland Road carried out their orders and delayed the British reinforcements from entering the city, wreaking havoc among the inexperienced British troops. The men were not in direct communication with headquarters and so did not receive any instructions. They used personal initiative and individual discretion in directing the battle.

The tactical planning employed by the Volunteers at Mount Street Bridge provided early warning of the advancing British forces. They engaged the enemy at long range and also deceived the attacking force as to the true location of the defences in the area. Many books written on the Rising praise the courage of the Irish Volunteers and their sacrifice to the cause; however, few, if any, praise their military skill.

The Volunteers were in training from the establishment of the organisation in 1913, and the officers who had been trained by the Fianna were well versed in military organisation and the use of weapons. Their training had prepared them for fighting in a built-up area and defending a chosen position. The Irish Volunteers were just that – volunteers dedicated to a cause they believed in, and they were willing to give their lives for that cause. They displayed excellent leadership and discipline at Mount Street and so had a considerable advantage over the inexperienced British troops.

A study of twenty-first century conflicts such as those in Iraq or Afghanistan reveals that tactics and strategies have changed very little from those deployed in Dublin in 1916. Wars today are not fought on open terrain but in cities, towns and villages. Tactics employed by modern armies still include frontal assaults, outflanking movements and ambushes.

Countries that believe they have supremacy over an adversary still rely on overwhelming their enemy with superior numbers or with advanced technology. Rapid movement of resources against the enemy results in a military tactic known as 'shock and awe'. This manoeuvre is intended to break the enemy's will to fight and affect them psychologically. Though this tactic has won many battles it has failed to win many wars. The occupation of a country by a superior force after an initial military confrontation often results in the outbreak of guerrilla warfare. The tactic employed here is one of attrition as ambushes and car bombings compete against counter-insurgency tactics.

This type of warfare was predicted by a Polish banker named Ivan Bloch as early as 1911. He stated that future conflicts would be wars of attrition in which defence would be the controlling aspect. In order to be victorious a side would have to contribute huge amounts of resources to overcome the enemy. It was only when the strain proved too much and one side capitulated that a successful outcome would be considered.

In the battle for Dublin in April 1916, the Irish Volunteers faced a force of 20,000 British soldiers by the end of Easter week. Many of the Volunteers' defences had withstood attacks by the crown forces and it was the use of heavy artillery and machine guns that forced them from their posts. Faced by overwhelming odds and ever-increasing civilian casualties, the Volunteers had to surrender. The battle of Mount Street, however, did not end in surrender but a tactical withdrawal by the survivors from their posts. The men of C Company had held their positions and carried out their instructions until ordered to withdraw.

The battle of Mount Street was a huge success for the Volunteers.

13

TODAY – LET US NOT BE FORGOTTEN

NÁ LIG SINN i nDEARMAD

A year afterwards, after my release from internment I stood in Glasnevin cemetery beside Michael's grave, which had been opened for the purpose of identity and I had a last glimpse of my leader and comrade in his stained, olive green uniform. Michael and Seán Cullen of Boland's Bakery Garrison and myself fired three revolver volleys over his grave.[62]

These words were spoken by James Grace, the survivor of 25 Northumberland Road. Having been released from prison in England he returned to Ireland and sought out the last resting place of his commanding officer and friend, Lieutenant Michael Malone. This gesture was a fitting tribute to a fallen comrade.

Commemoration and remembrance of the 1916 rebellion and the men and women who took part has for many years been extirpated from official records. The Rising laid the groundwork for events that not only led to Irish independence but to Ireland's recognition as the country that signalled the final chapter of the British empire.

From his prison cell in Lewes jail Éamon de Valera wrote to Michael Malone's mother:

> I do not think I ever got a gift which affected me so much as your box of shamrocks on St Patrick's Day – indeed I should have said I am sure. For what gift could be so affecting as that of a box of shamrocks from an Irish mother, on behalf of her patriot son, to a comrade whose duty it was to bid him take that post, in the defence of which he so gloriously fell. No wonder that Ireland is still unconquered. Surely that cause must be blessed, for which young men are willing to sacrifice their lives just budding with the promises of the future, and mothers the fulfilment of the dreams first dreamt by their cradles … Michael did deeds which will be on record for ever – accomplished in a few hours what other men fail to accomplish in a life full of years. This Easter from his place in paradise he sees us still struggling though this valley of tears … His fate is one for envy not sorrow. E de Valera.[63]

The veterans who took part in the battle of Mount Street continued the struggle against the British crown during the war for Irish independence and then, like many Irish Volunteers, fought again for a republic during the bitter conflict of the Civil War.

The men who defended Mount Street Bridge are remembered by a number of statues and plaques in the Ballsbridge area of Dublin. Near the Royal Dublin Society there is a statue to commemorate the men of the 3rd battalion of the Irish Volunteers who were positioned in the area and commanded by Éamon de Valera. A second statue stands beside the bridge at Mount Street, commemorating the small band of men that defended this approach to the city. A plaque at 25 Northumberland Road remembers Lieutenant Michael Malone. In the aftermath of Ireland's struggle for independence and its civil war, individual groups sought to remember their fallen comrades in their own private way. The 1916 rebellion had failed, but, like many rebellions before, had succeeded in encouraging future generations to continue the quest for independence.

In 1934 Éamon de Valera, who had entered the political arena, warned republicans that an armed struggle by any Irish citizen was not acceptable unless it was in defence of the state and was sanctioned by the government of the people of Ireland. However, politicians could not ignore the past sacrifice of 1916, and those who were killed and executed were given cult status. As the years passed, military parades were orchestrated by a succession of governments and created fervour among the people. These events were small to begin with but grew in popularity as the years progressed.

In Britain, Remembrance Day recalls those British and allied servicemen and women who died in two world wars. Originally called Armistice Day, the first of these ceremonies took place on 11 November 1919. As the years progressed the event was commemorated by a two-minute silence, church services and parades to newly erected memorials. In Ireland these events became controversial following the establishment of the Irish Free State, and the 200,000 Irishmen who took part in the war from 1914 to 1918 remained a private memory for those who had served or who had lost loved ones during that conflict.

The Sherwood Foresters who lost their lives as they assaulted the positions on Mount Street and Northumberland Road are listed as 'killed at home' in official war records.[64] The regiment has a memorial at Crich in England to honour its war dead. Sadly, in Ireland many of the men of the regiment are buried in forgotten graveyards throughout Dublin city. The Commonwealth War Graves Commission has erected many headstones to the men who were killed in action during the battle of Mount Street, but others lie in forgotten graveyards, their headstones damaged, a distant memory of a battle lost. Some of those who fell were taken back to their home county in England and buried in local graveyards where they could be tended by their families and loved ones. Too many had died that April day in 1916 to a force of seventeen Irish men, and the British army sought to forget this unpleasant chapter in its history. The real heroes were on the Western Front and it was felt that it was best to bury the men of the Sherwood Foresters in Ireland and hopefully forget about the disaster that befell the regiment during the battle of Mount Street Bridge. The British soldiers who were killed in action in Dublin in 1916 are not remembered or commemorated separately. They take their place among the fallen of the Great War, with the battle for Dublin a fading memory, reflected on their worn headstones.

During the commemoration of the fiftieth anniversary of the Rising, Tom Walsh wrote of the Sherwood Forester regiment: 'They were brave men and, I must say, clean fighters.'[65]

As the decades passed, successive governments tried to forget that Ireland's independence was brought about through armed struggle, and attempted to scale down the commemorative events around the country. In Ireland this was not the first time that people tried to forget the past. Many also attempted to erase the memory of almost 200,000 Irishmen who joined the British army to fight during the Great War.

The Irish Volunteers who fought at Mount Street Bridge received recognition in the form of a statue and plaque. However, the individuals and their sacrifice in one of the most successful battles in Irish history have largely been forgotten. The leaders of the rebellion gained infamy following their executions in Kilmainham gaol in May 1916 but the ordinary Volunteers, both men and women, have remained faceless for almost a century. It is only since 1954 that a military parade at Easter to commemorate the rebellion has become an annual event in Ireland. This parade passes the General Post Office in Dublin, the former headquarters of the provisional government of 1916.

Over the years the commemorations grew in size and the military parade to mark the fiftieth anniversary in 1966 was a spectacular affair. However, as the troubles in the north intensified in the latter half of that decade, the commemorations tended to become more subdued; governments sought to distance themselves from 1916 as Ireland took its place in the newly developing Europe. The veterans who took part in the parades began to dwindle in number; many passed on and others refused to take part, believing that they had become marginalised and excluded from a country that had entered a new phase of political advancement with membership of the European Union.[66]

Today, both the 1916 rebellion and the Great War are remembered in a series of ceremonies. These are attended by dignitaries from both the republic and Northern Ireland, bringing an end to years of political amnesia and creating a bridge between the past and the future.

EPILOGUE

Today if you stroll down Northumberland Road towards Mount Street Bridge you will find little evidence of the battle that took place. It is impossible to imagine the carnage and death visited on this stretch of road on that spring morning in April 1916. The remembrance plaque on the wall of number 25 and the monument on the bridge could be easily missed unless you look carefully. The city's regeneration is eroding the memories of Easter 1916 as buildings are replaced and modern facades cover our past.

The headstones in the graveyard at the Royal Hospital Kilmainham still lie undisturbed, neglected and forgotten. Lieutenant Michael Malone's body lies in Glasnevin cemetery, Dublin, a small simple stone located in the republican plot, overlooked by more famous names in Irish history; perhaps he too has become a forgotten soldier.

The story of the battle of Mount Street Bridge is tragic yet heroic. What is more tragic, however, is the failure to remember this episode in Irish and British history. The names of the men who participated in the epic battle have been consigned to dusty annals, a page in an archive or a paragraph in a book. We must try to remember the inscription on the Menin Gate at Ypres in Belgium:

> They shall grow not old, as we that are left grow old. Age shall not weary them, nor the years condemn. At the going down of the sun and in the morning we will remember them.[67]

In Ireland the inscription in the Garden of Remembrance for the Irish Volunteers reads:

> In the darkness and despair we saw a vision. We lit the light of hope and it was not extinguished. In the desert of discouragement we saw a vision. We planted the tree of valour and it blossomed.
>
> In the winter of bondage we saw a vision. We melted the snow of lethargy and the river of resurrection flowed from it.
>
> We sent our vision aswim like a swan on a river. The vision became a reality. Winter became summer. Bondage became freedom. And this we left to you as our inheritance.
>
> O generations of freedom remember us. The generations of the vision.[68]

They shall be remembered.

Notes

1   Nowlan, K.B., *The Making of 1916, Studies in the History of the Rising* (Dublin, Hely Thom Ltd, 1967).

2   Rees, R., *Ireland 1905–25: Vol. 1 Text & Historiography* (Newtownards, Colourpoint Books, 1998).

3   Nowlan, *The Making of 1916*.

4   Doyle, J., Witness Statement File No. S. 709, W.S 127 (Bureau of Military History 1913–1921, Dublin).

5   *Ibid.*

6   Walsh, T., *Irish Press* Supplement, 9 April 1966.

7   Kilberd, D., *1916 Rebellion Handbook* (Dublin, The Mourne River Press, 1998).

8   *Ibid.*

9   Walsh, T., *Irish Press*

10   W. C. Oates, *The Sherwood Foresters in the Great War 1/7th, 2/7th, 3/7th, 1914–1918* (Nottingham, J & H Bell Ltd, 1920).

11   W. C. Oates, *The Sherwood Foresters in the Great War 1914–1918, 2/8th battalion* (Nottingham, J & H Bell Ltd, 1921).

12   W. C. Oates, *The Sherwood Foresters in the Great War 1/7th, 2/7th, 3/7th, 1914–1918.*

13   Sheane, R., 'Five Days Experiences, during the "Sinn Féin" Rising of 1916', *Wicklow Historical Society*, Vol. 3, No. 1 (July 2002).

14   Walsh, T., *Irish Press*.

15   Caulfield, M., *The Easter Rebellion* (Dublin, Gill & Macmillan, 1995).

16   Sheane, 'Five Days Experiences, during the "Sinn Féin" Rising of 1916'.

17   Walsh, T., *Irish Press*.

18   Donnelly, S., *They Shall Not Pass, Statement on the Battle of Mount Street* (Unpublished, University College Dublin).

19   Walsh, T., *Irish Press*.

20   Gerrard, E., *Irish Times*, 24 April 1916.

21   Caulfield, *The Easter Rebellion*.

22   McCann, J., *War By The Irish* (Tralee, The Kerryman Ltd, 1946).

23   Lyons, G., *An t-Óglac*, 24 April, 1926.

24   Oates, *The Sherwood Foresters in the Great War 1914–1918, 2/8th battalion*.

25   *Ibid*.

26   *Ibid*.

27   *Ibid*.

28   O'Connor, Cmdt. J., *The Capuchin Annual* (Dublin, Dollard Printing, 1966).

29   Caulfield, *The Easter Rebellion*.

30   Oates, *The Sherwood Foresters in the Great War 1914–1918, 2/8th battalion*.

31   *Ibid*.

32   Lyons, G., *An t-Óglac*, 24 April, 1926.

33   McCann, *War By The Irish*.

34   Walsh, T., *Irish Press*.

35   Oates, *The Sherwood Foresters in the Great War 1/7th, 2/7th, 3/7th, 1914–1918*.

36   Walsh, T., *Irish Press*.

37   Oates, *The Sherwood Foresters in the Great War 1/7th, 2/7th, 3/7th, 1914–1918*.

38   Walsh, T., *Irish Press*.

39   Caulfield, *The Easter Rebellion*.

40   O'Mahony, S., *Frongoch University of Revolution* (Dublin, Elo Press, 1995).

41   War Office Files, 35/67.

42   *Ibid.*

43   Dickson, A.A., Imperial War Museum Transcript (Imperial War Museum, London, 1998).

44   *Ibid.*

45   Barton, B., *From Behind a Closed Door* (Belfast, Blackstaff Press, 2003).

46   Aloysius, F., *Memories of Easter Week, 1916* (Dublin, Allen Library), from the personal recollections of Fr Aloysius, published in part in *La Vie De Pearse* (Louis N. Le Roux) translated by Desmond Ryan, and in *The Capuchin Annual*, 1966.

47   Maxwell, J.G., *Irish Times*, 25 May 1916.

48   Kilberd, D., *1916 Rebellion Handbook* (Dublin, The Mourne River Press, 1998).

49   Maxwell, J.G., *Irish Times*, 25 May 1916.

50   O'Brien, C.B., Simon Donnelly statement (University College Dublin Archives).

51   W.O. 903/19 PT 2

52   Dickson, A.A., Imperial War Museum Transcript (Imperial War Museum, London, 1998).

53   Maconchy, E.W.S.K., 7908 – 62 –1 (National Army Museum, London, 1920).

54   Mac Lochlainn P.F., *Last Words* (Dublin, Dúchas, 1990).

55   Doyle, J., Witness Statement File No. S. 709, W.S 127 (Bureau of Military History 1913–1921, Dublin).

56   Nowlan, *The Making of 1916, Studies in the History of the Rising*.

57   Holmes, R., *The Oxford Companion to Military History* (Oxford, Oxford University Press, 2001).

58   Hally, Col. P.J., 'The Easter 1916 Rising in Dublin: The Military Aspects' (Dublin, The Irish Sword, 1966).

59   Rumbelow, D., *The Houndsditch Murders & the Siege of Sidney Street* (London, St Martin's Press / Macmillan, 1973).

60   Oates, *The Sherwood Foresters in the Great War 1/7th, 2/7th, 3/7th, 1914–1918.*

61   Lyons, G., *An t-Óglac*, 24 April, 1926.

62   Grace, J., *Irish Press*, de Valera, E., Papers (University College Dublin).

63   De Valera, E., Papers (University College Dublin).

64   CD Rom, *Soldiers Died in the Great War, Version 2* (Sussex, Naval & Military Press, 2004).

65   Walsh, T., *Irish Press.*

66   Walker, B., *Past & Present: History, Identity and Politics in Ireland* (Belfast, Institute of Irish Studies, Queen's University, 2000).

67   Menin Gate inscription, Ypres, Belgium.

68   Uistín Liam Mac, 'We Saw A Vision', Garden of Remembrance, Dublin.

Index

Symbols

20 Delahunty Buildings 95
23 Northumberland Road 79
25 Northumberland Road 19, 22, 24, 25, 39, 41, 43, 44, 45, 46, 47, 49, 54, 56, 62, 63, 66, 67, 82, 83, 96, 108, 111, 113, 117
28 Northumberland Road 24, 44

A

Act of Union 11, 12
Aloysius, Father 89
Armistice Day 114
Aylesbury Jail 87

B

Baggot Street 40, 44, 46, 53, 54, 104
Baggot Street Bridge 40, 44, 46, 53
Ballsbridge 19, 35, 37, 38, 42, 53, 91, 92, 113
Baltinglass 97
Beggars Bush barracks 19, 24, 28, 50, 51, 59
Belgium 30, 36, 101
Blackrock 37, 40
Bloch, Ivan 109
Boland's bakery 19, 22, 24, 27, 28, 40, 48, 51, 79, 96, 106, 107, 111
Booth, Private J.E. 63

Brown, Lieutenant Montague Bernard 67
Browning, Mr F.H. 23
Brugha, Cathal 81
Byrne, Daniel 20, 28
Byrne, Paddy 19, 25

C

Carlton, Brigadier General L.B. 35, 37
Carrisbrooke House 19, 40, 43
Carson, Sir Edward 13
Casement, Sir Roger 31
Caulfield, Max 55
Ceannt, Commandant Éamonn 15, 80
Christian, William 20
Churchill, Winston 102
Citizen Army 14, 89
Civil War 97, 112
Clanwilliam House 19, 20, 21, 22, 25, 27, 28, 29, 38, 44, 45, 46, 47, 48, 49, 50, 55, 56, 57, 58, 62, 66, 67, 68, 70, 71, 74, 77, 78, 82, 83, 96, 104, 107, 108
Clanwilliam Place 19
Clanwilliam Terrace 48, 66
Clarke, Joe 20, 64, 83, 97
Clarke, Tom 15
Clery, Corporal 23
Commonwealth War Graves Commission 114
Connolly, James 14, 15, 40, 105

Cooper, Bandmaster 79
Cooper, Captain L.L. 35, 53, 70
Cooper, Robert 20
Cooper, Sergeant R.M. 92
Craig, James 13
Crowley, Eugene 98
Cullen, May 39
Cullen, Sean 111
Cumann na mBan 40
Cumming, Sergeant Major T. 92
Curragh 100
Cursham, Captain F. 70, 74
Curtis, Lieutenant 74

D

Daffen, Lieutenant Harold
        Charles 66, 67
Dalkey 57
Dartmoor prison 97
de Valera, Éamon 19, 21, 51, 96,
        97, 98, 106, 107, 112, 113
Dickson, Captain Arthur Annan
        56, 86, 87, 88, 94, 95
Dietrichsen, Adjutant Captain
        Frederick 36, 37, 43, 91
Dietrichsen, Beatrice 36, 37
Distinguished Conduct Medal 92
Distinguished Service Order 92
Dixie, Sergeant Major 74
Dodder River 42
Donnelly, Captain Simon 18,
        19, 28, 48, 49, 51, 71, 73,
        96, 97
Donnybrook 35
O'Donoghue, Adjutant Denis 20
Doyle, Jimmy 20, 25, 27, 39, 68,
        69, 71, 72, 75, 76, 82, 97
Doyle, Patrick 20, 28, 29, 39, 69,

70, 75, 83
Doyle, Seamus 48
Dublin Castle 100
Dun, Sir Patrick 57

E

Earlsfort Terrace 18
Elm Park Bombing School of
        Instruction 53, 62

F

Fane, Battalion Lieutenant
        Colonel Cecil 36, 38, 43,
        44, 46, 50, 51, 53, 60, 92
Foster, Lieutenant William 43,
        66, 70, 74, 76, 77
Four Courts 106
France 11, 14, 22, 30, 34, 36, 94,
        95, 101
Friend, Major General C.H. 100,
        103
Frongoch Prison 83

G

Gaelic League 12
Gamble, Colour Quarter Master
        Sergeant 51
Garden of Remembrance 118
General Post Office 106, 116
Georgius Rex 22, 24
Gerrard, Captain E. 51, 52
Glasnevin cemetery 83, 111, 117
Grace, Bridget 39
Grace, James 19, 23, 24, 25, 39,
        40, 43, 45, 46, 47, 54, 56,
        63, 64, 67, 82, 111
Grand Canal 19, 28, 38, 50, 51,

60, 79, 104

Grand Canal Street 19, 28, 50, 51, 79, 104

Great Brunswick Street 106

Guilfoyle, Joseph 51

Guilfoyle, Lieutenant John 24

H

Haddington Road 22, 25, 43, 44, 45, 50, 54, 59, 65, 67, 91

Hall, Reverend 57

Hanchette Hyland, Mr C. 95

Hanson, Major H. 35, 44, 46, 47, 49, 54, 61

Harris, Major 22

Hartshorn, Second Lieutenant 49

Hawken, Lieutenant William Victor 54

Hayter, Mr 95

Heathcote, Major Harold 86

Heuston, Seán 95

Hewitt, Lieutenant H.A. 36, 70, 74

Hill, Private J. 92

Hobson, Bulmer 15

Holyhead 32

House of Commons 12, 13

Howard, Redmond 57

Howth 20, 21

Hutchinson, Corporal H. 63

I

Imperial War Museum 95

Irish Citizen Army 14

Irish Free State 114

Irish Parliamentary Party 12, 14

Irish Republican Brotherhood (IRB) 15, 16, 17

Irish Transport and General Workers' Union (ITGWU) 13, 14

J

Jacob's biscuit factory 106

Jeffares, Captain 53, 62

K

Kane, Mrs Elizabeth 95

Kavanagh, James 20

Kavanagh, Seamus 48

Keogh, Dr Myles 57

Kilmainham 9, 35, 56, 80, 81, 84, 85, 86, 87, 88, 89, 90, 94, 95, 97, 116, 117

Kingstown (Dún Laoghaire) 22, 31, 32, 34, 35, 37, 38, 40, 91, 100

L

Lad Lane barracks 65

Lamb, Second Lieutenant 49

Lansdowne Road 23, 59

Larkin, James 13

Lewes jail 112

Lieutenant Colonel WC Oates 32

Love Lane 81

Lowe, Brigadier General W.H.M. 59, 60, 61, 100, 103

Lower Grand Canal Street 19

Lower Mount Street 91

M

MacNeill, Eoin 15, 16, 17, 18, 28, 97, 106

Maconchy, Brigadier Colonel
Ernest William Stuart
King 32, 35, 38, 59, 60, 61
65, 78, 81, 95
Major Hanson 44, 46, 49, 54, 61
Mallin, Michael 95
Malone, Lieutenant Michael 18,
19, 21, 22, 23, 24, 25, 27,
29, 39, 40, 41, 43, 44, 45,
46, 47, 54, 56, 63, 64, 67,
83, 98, 106, 107, 111, 112,
113, 117
Malone, William 22
Markievicz, Countess 87
Marrowbone Lane distillery 80
Martyn, Captain M.C. 79, 81, 93
Marx, Joseph 102
Maxwell, General Sir John 91,
93, 94
McCann, Fr 58
McDermott, Sean 15
McGrath, James 20
McNevin, Fr 58
Melville, Captain A.B. Leslie 70
Menin Gate 118
Merrion Square 79, 82, 91
Military Medal 93
Monkstown 28
Mountjoy prison 86, 87, 88
Murphy, Dick 29, 39, 70, 75
Murphy, Richard 28, 83
Murphy, William Martin 13

N

National Museum of Ireland 98

Nolan, Louisa 57, 93
Northumberland Road 19, 20, 22,
23, 24, 25, 37, 39, 40, 41,
43, 44, 45, 47, 49, 53, 54,
55, 56, 58, 60, 62, 63, 65,
66, 67, 74, 79, 82, 83, 91,
95, 96, 103, 104, 106, 107,
108, 111, 113, 114, 117

O

O'Brien, Dr C.B. 57, 93
O'Donoghue, Adjutant Denis 25,
27, 48
Oates, Lieutenant Colonel W.
Coape 35, 38, 59, 61, 65,
74, 80

P

Paris Commune 101
Parochial Hall 19, 20, 24, 39, 45,
47, 49, 55, 56, 62, 64, 66,
83, 108
Pearse, Patrick 15, 24, 96
Pearse, William 95
Pembroke Cottages 73
Pembroke Road 19, 40
Pembroke Town Hall 38, 60, 61,
79
Percy Lane 61, 62, 64, 67, 71
Percy Place 46, 49, 61, 67, 69,
79, 96
Perry, Lieutenant Percy Claude 48
102
Piatkov, Peter (Peter the Painter)
21, 102
Pierce, Kathleen 57
Plunkett, Countess 87

Plunkett, Joseph 15, 95, 105
Portobello barracks 80
Pragnell, Captain Frank 35, 43, 44, 54, 61, 62

Q

Quibell, Captain A.H. 59, 66, 70, 74, 76, 92

R

Rathmines 80
Rayner, Major 36, 43, 45, 77, 92
Redmond, John 14
Remembrance Day 114
Reynolds, George 20, 21, 22, 25, 27, 28, 29, 39, 46, 49, 50, 55, 57, 58, 59, 62, 67, 68, 69, 70, 71, 72, 75, 76, 83
Richmond barracks 85, 86, 87
Ringsend 21
Roberts' yard 19, 48, 49, 51, 56, 62, 71, 73, 96
Ronan, Willie 20, 39, 69, 70, 71, 75, 76, 81, 97
Rowe, Michael 19, 25
Royal Dublin Horse Society 79
Royal Dublin Showground 96
Royal Dublin Society (RDS) 37, 42, 113
Royal Hospital 9, 35, 80, 81, 117

S

Sandbach, Major General A.E. 25
Schoolhouse 19, 20, 25, 27, 38, 46, 47, 48, 50, 55, 60, 66, 70, 71, 73, 79, 80, 103, 104
Scovell, Captain 28

Scully, Miss 47
Serpentine Avenue 59
Shaw, Sir Frederick 50, 51
Sheane, Richard 37, 42
Shelbourne hotel 29
Shelbourne Road 22
Sinn Féin 12, 20, 98
Sinn Féin Bank 20
Sir Patrick Dun's hospital 57, 62, 80
Snowdin, F. 92
South Circular Road 80
South Dublin Union 80, 81, 106
South Lotts Road 51
Stephens Place 82
St George 92
Stillorgan 35
St Mary's Church 50
St Mary's Road 43, 59, 65
St Stephen's Green 29, 40, 106
Sunday Independent 16
Svaars, Fritz 102

T

They Shall Not Pass 97
Towlson, Company Sergeant Major 49
Trinity College 22, 38, 79, 91, 92, 100

V

Vane, Major Sir Francis 80

W

Wakefield prison 83
Walsh, James 28, 46, 47, 49, 50, 55, 56, 69, 71, 76, 81

Walsh, Mrs 82
Walsh, Tom 28, 38, 39, 46, 47, 49,
        50, 55, 56, 69, 70, 71, 75,
        76, 81, 82, 115
War Office 84, 100
Warren, Corporal 66
Warrington Place 67, 69, 72
Waters, Richard 28
Western Front 30, 32, 102, 115
Whitehead, Captain H.M. 85
Wilson, Miss 20, 21
Wilson family 72
Wright, Captain H.C. 35, 50,
        51, 59

Y

Young, Brigadier J. 84